BOOMERS

BOOMERS

The Cold-War Generation Grows Up

\\\\\|//

VICTOR D. BROOKS

Chicago · Ivan R. Dee · 2009

www.ivanrdee.com

Library of Congress Cataloging-in-Publication Data:
Brooks, Victor.
   Boomers : the cold war generation grows up / Victor D. Brooks.
      p. cm.
   Includes bibliographical references and index.
   ISBN 978-1-56663-724-4 (cloth : alk. paper)
   1. Baby boom generation—United States. 2. United States—History—
1945– I. Title.
   HN57.B655 2009
   305.240973'09045—dc22   2008052622

For James T. Kane

PREFACE

ONLY SECONDS after noisemakers and fireworks welcomed the New Year of 1946, a seemingly minor event occurred fewer than two miles from the birthplace of American nationhood. As millions of people celebrated the first full year of world peace since 1939, the wife of a navy machinist gave birth to a daughter at Philadelphia Naval Hospital. The arrival of Kathleen Casey rated a short feature in the hospital newsletter but initially seemed to have little significance beyond her immediate family. Twelve months later, Kathleen's arrival would gain rising importance for the simple reason that more than 3.5 million other babies had followed her into American households in that one year, a number that dwarfed the infants born in both the 1920s and 1930s. Confident predictions that this surge was a one-year postwar phenomenon seemed to unravel when 3.8 million new babies arrived in 1947, and were shattered when the count passed 4 million the next year. Gradually, as maternity wards set new records with the arrival of each new decade, terms such as "spike" and "bubble" gave way to longer-term labels of "Population Explosion" and the "Baby Boom." The physical manifestation of this new reality in twentieth-century American culture emerged in Washington, D.C., in the lobby of the Commerce Department. A supremely modern version of a tolling bell, a newly installed Census Clock, flashed multicolored lights every 7.5 seconds to record the birth of a new American citizen, a frequency that would not slow until the end of 1964. When the Baby Boom was over, 76 million children were dominating communities from Levittown, New York, to Pasadena, California, and renewing Americans' sense of optimism and purpose.

This book is a chronicle of the "great invasion" of the United States in the period between the end of World War II and the close of the 1960s. It was a unique kind of invasion—noisy and occasionally even threatening, but also fascinating and even enjoyable for adults and children alike. A national psyche that seemed tentative and frightened during a depression that dominated the 1930s, and feared a resumption of the same after the guns of World War II were stilled, was prodded into cheerful renewal by an army of young people who brought prosperity in their wake. This is the narrative of a postwar world where, if far too many children experienced the sting of racial, religious, ethnic, or gender bias and discrimination, the stage was also set for a more equitable, more sensitive, and more caring childhood for many other young people.

The story begins with the marriage and parenting activities of the "Greatest Generation" after World War II and ends with the tumultuous events in the late sixties. There are a number of fine books on the Boomer experience, ranging from Todd Gitlin's *The Sixties* to Tom Brokaw's *Boom*, but I have attempted to consider the period from new perspectives.

I have perused a great many published books on the era but also much less commonly utilized sources, including popular magazines ranging from *Life* and *Look* to *Parents* and *Jack and Jill*, to DVDs, videotapes, and even kinescopes of period television programs and films. I have also conducted hundreds of interviews of Boomers, seeking informality and free-flowing responses, which revealed cultural trends and offered a spontaneity that could not have been accomplished with more formal questions and quantitative analysis. This process was furthered by the enthusiasm of individuals or groups of Boomers to relate their special childhood experiences, which then allowed me to construct the larger picture.

My research and the extensive conversations with Boomers have prompted a number of the focal points of this book—for example, what people of the era wore and ate, their home environments and level of technology, and relationships between parents and children and between siblings. Boomer children were also enormously influenced by the explosion of popular culture and mass media in the fifties and sixties, and in turn they influenced these trends to an even larger degree. This is a recurring theme of the book. The Boomers attended school in larger numbers and for longer periods than any previous generation; educational issues occupied an important portion of their childhood experiences. Finally, a significant segment of the Boomer generation grew up at the peak of the East-West confrontation that we remember as the cold war, which paralleled the impact of the Great Depression on children of the 1930s and World War II on young people of the 1940s. The cold war could mean the terror of the Cuban Missile Crisis, the alarm of the Sputnik launch, or the elation of Apollo XI, but it was always present in some sense, from the yellow signs that directed students to school fallout shelters to the *Life* magazine articles that compared student life in American and Soviet schools.

A personal acknowledgment: I was born early in the second year of the Baby Boom as the oldest of four children of a Catholic Democratic mother who had been a secretary and was now a full-time homemaker, and a Protestant Republican father who had served as a major in the army air corps during World War II and was in the process of becoming a college psychology professor. For my first twelve years I lived in a suburb of Philadelphia in a 1930s-era twin (semidetached) house. Our neighborhood was composed primarily, but not exclusively, of relatively equal numbers of white Catholic and Protestant families with a significant minority of Jewish households and a smattering of relatively recently arrived Latinos from Guatemala and Asians from Taiwan. In the twenty houses on our street lived families with three to six children; just one family had only two children, and an older couple had no young children.

The crowded living conditions of six people in a small, one-bathroom, attached home prompted subsequent moves to a 1920s stone Tudor, a brand-new 1960-model split-level, and finally a 1964-model spacious colonial on a large lot. Frequent sleepovers with relatives who lived in Levittown-style ranches and Victorian-era single-family houses provided an opportunity for me to experience most of the major housing arrangements of the Boomer era.

My diversity of housing experiences was matched by a variety of educational venues, including a parochial elementary school, a public high school, a Catholic college, and an Ivy League university. Each of these experiences gradually added to my wonder at the complexity of my Boomer generation, as my peers at each school had both much in common with and yet major differences in outlook from those in the other institutions I had experienced. The fascination of trying to understand the role of children in an adult world was substantially expanded when I became a single parent soon after the birth of my third son. As many single parents understand, the merging of maternal and parental roles produces grand opportunities along with daunting challenges. In the case of my three highly verbal children, this meant not only endless questions about the world in which they lived but also questions about the world in which *I* grew up. Nothing prompts a book about childhood in the past better than answering the questions of children in the present.

My adult support for this project came from a variety of sources. I wish to thank James Marten of Marquette University and Ivan Dee for their confidence in my proposal for this book. Dr. John Johannes, vice president for academic affairs; Rev. Kail Ellis, O.S.A., dean of the College of Arts and Sciences; and Dr. Connie Titone, chair of the Department of Education and Human Services, have given me great support and encouragement in the Villanova academic community. Anne Feldman of our departmental staff not only is one of the few people who can translate my handwriting but also provides stylistic suggestions that have always improved the text. Graduate students Amanda Meltz and Christina Beebe joined in the pick-and-shovel work of interlibrary loans and proofreading.

Finally, I wish to dedicate this work to my recently deceased uncle, James T. Kane, who spent his late adolescence in the front lines of the Korean War, preventing a bloody conflict from turning into a nuclear war. Corporal Kane and many others like him were too young to be part of the Greatest Generation of World War II and too old to be Boomers. Yet their sacrifices allowed the Boomer generation to spend their childhoods in relative peace and security while ensuring that the magic of their youth could be passed to their own children and grandchildren.

CONTENTS

BOOMERS

PROLOGUE

WEDNESDAY, August 15, 1945, dawned sunny and hot across vast reaches of the forty-eight states that formed the American republic. Paperboys cycled on their delivery rounds, barely noticing the seemingly endless succession of small blue-starred banners in living-room windows that reminded passersby that one or more occupants of that home were active members of the armed forces of the United States. An ever-increasing number of the blue stars had been replaced by gold ones, a silent reminder that a family member had made the supreme sacrifice in the service of his or her country. Nearly 400,000 windows now held gold star banners in this 1,347th day since the Day of Infamy at Pearl Harbor had plunged the United States into World War II.

As the sun rose higher, housewives and mothers made their daily excursions to grocery stores, butcher shops, and clothing stores, carefully clutching multicolored booklets of ration coupons that largely determined the eating habits, clothing styles, and transportation arrangements of every American over thirty days old. Butchers informed customers what meats were available that day, grocers apologized

3

for the absence of several varieties of canned fruits and veg-
etables, and restaurant patrons breathed a sigh of relief that
today was not a meatless Tuesday or Friday so that a relatively complete menu was available.

Housewives were not the only people on the street. Children walked, ran, or roller-skated with the carefree abandon
of pupils on summer vacation; teenage girls in bobby sox
and saddle shoes playfully teased boys in baggy pants and
crumpled fedoras; older men sat contentedly in the sunshine in the town park or played checkers with cronies. Yet a
casual visitor would soon notice that this picturesque scene
included very few young men. Millions of young Americans
were either overseas in war zones, preparing for combat in
training camps, or working in the never-shuttered factories
that made the weapons for a conflict that General Dwight
Eisenhower had recently named the Great Crusade.

The 130 million Americans of 1945 who were living in
this time of high drama and significant personal sacrifice
were part of a society that seemed incredibly modern and
fast moving, compared even to the relatively recent turn of
the century just four decades earlier. Daily newspapers, lavishly illustrated magazines, and theatrical films and newsreels were major elements in a sensory bombardment that
addressed the entire enterprise called the "War Effort." But
the most intimate yet universal source of knowledge was the
radio, which had become the centerpiece of virtually every
family's living room. Whether it took the form of an ornate
mahogany console with rows of illuminated dials or an inexpensive table model with a few functional knobs, a radio
was the lifeline to the outside world as authoritative, well-
modulated voices kept listeners informed of the dramatic,

sometimes tragic, events that marked a nation engaged in total war.

In the preceding twelve years, even before the terrible news of Pearl Harbor in 1941, the most recognizable voice on the radio was the melodious, confident diction of President Franklin Delano Roosevelt, who, through his "fireside chats," seemed to become an additional family member in the parlor. Just as the Nazi Reich entered its final days, a radio voice trembling with emotion announced that the commander-in-chief had died in Warm Springs, Georgia. A grief-stricken nation mourned its fallen leader, even as it heard of the death of Hitler and the surrender of the German Wehrmacht.

A new voice now entered American living rooms—the flat, businesslike cadence of former Missouri senator Harry S. Truman, who was catapulted from relative obscurity into the Oval Office. Thus when network announcers notified their audience that the president would address the nation at 2 P.M., Eastern War Time, on this summer afternoon, the voice that followed still seemed a bit strange, especially to the millions of American children who had known only one president in their living memory.

Harry Truman may have sounded a bit too abrupt to be pictured sitting by the family fireside, but the message he delivered was likely the best news in the lifetimes of most Americans. After almost four years of war, 400,000 American deaths, and 50 million worldwide fatalities, the Emperor of Japan had accepted Allied surrender terms, and peace was about to return to the United States. Twelve million American servicemen and servicewomen would now return to civilian life and experience every conceivable type of reunion, from family picnics to engagement parties to wedding celebrations. Marines occupying the bleak landscape of Iwo Jima, airmen stationed on bomber bases in England, sailors serving on destroyers in the Pacific Ocean, soldiers manning foxholes against the last sporadic Japanese resistance on Okinawa, and nurses captured on Bataan and held in Manila internment camps for three years were all coming home. Some would come home to spouses and children, others to fiancées, boyfriends, or girlfriends. Many had met someone special during their service activities. However these young American men and women had developed relationships that led to marriage, they would produce a second legacy beyond winning World War II and securing the American way of life and the dreams that accompanied it. During the next two decades this "Greatest Generation" would in turn create a new generation of almost 76 million boys and girls who, despite enormous differences in lifestyle, education, and attitude, would share membership in a group that would soon be called simply the "Baby Boomers." America would never again be quite the same.

1

GENESIS OF THE BABY BOOM

NEW YEAR'S DAY 1946 represented more than the usual festive celebrations that mark the transition of one year to the next. For the first time in seven years there was neither war nor the threat of war on the horizon, and now something other than military campaigns might capture the public's attention. A nation that had just steered through the treacherous shoals of a global conflict now found itself free to look farther back and farther forward for inspiration. One of the first news stories of 1946 was the 81st annual encampment of 67 Union Army veterans in Cleveland, where 102-year-old Robert Ripley of New York was elected commander-in-chief with a mandate to invite Confederate veterans to a joint reunion that summer.

Despite the eight decades that separated the American Civil War from the 1940s, tangible links to the conflict remained. During their childhoods, many of the returning World War II veterans had met Civil War participants. The wife of Gen. James Longstreet, Robert E. Lee's deputy at Gettysburg, was photographed riding in the back of a convertible at an Independence Day celebration, and Lt. Gen.

Simon Bolivar Buckner, commander of American forces in the battle of Okinawa and the most senior general to die in combat, was the son of Gen. Simon Bolivar Buckner, Sr., one of Ulysses S. Grant's closest friends at West Point and the first Confederate commander to surrender to the future Union commanding general. Older men and women still regaled wide-eyed children with stories of glimpses of Abraham Lincoln or Jefferson Davis, or even early memories of life as a slave.

Yet if America was still tethered to links with the Civil War era and nostalgic aspects of nineteenth-century life, an equally powerful attraction was the world of the twenty-first century that lay just over the horizon. The January 1946 issue of a national news magazine followed an article on Civil War veterans with a feature on the "Great Electro Mechanical Brain," describing MIT's follow-up to the University of Pennsylvania's breakthrough ENIAC "differential analyzer," with its computing machine that "advances science by freeing it from the pick and shovel work of mathematics." The new mechanical brain in Cambridge, Massachusetts, used two thousand vacuum tubes and two hundred miles of electrical wire in one hundred tons of hardware and metal that could solve in thirty minutes a problem that would take human scientists more than ten hours to complete. The four members of ENIAC's technical crew fed data to the machine that "could advance the frontiers of knowledge by liberating scientists from everyday equations for more creative work."

The exciting world of the "Atomic Age" future was a feature of current advertising. An early 1946 ad for the Hotel Pennsylvania illustrates the New York City of the twenty-first century with futuristic helicopters landing businessmen on the hotel roof. The copy insists that "many things are sure to change our lives in the new era of a new century. However, whether you come by helicopter or jet car, the Hotel Pennsylvania will never serve concentrated food pills as even in the future, we will still have full and robust meals."

Somewhere between the quaintness of the gaslight era and the excitement of the looming 21st century stood a real world into which 76 million babies would be born over the next 18 years. This America held tantalizing glimpses of the society we know today yet had been shaped substantially by the war and the depression decade of the 1930s. Compared to the fashion standards of twenty-first-century society, for example, most midcentury men, women, and to some extent children dressed much more formally, with propriety often trumping comfort.

The young men who would become the fathers of Boomer children included a large percentage for whom dress shirts, dress shoes, neckties, coats, and even dress hats were required wear—from work to PTA meetings to religious worship and even to summer promenades on resort boardwalks and piers. Men who worked in strenuous jobs, on assembly lines and loading docks, might be seen wearing neckties under their coveralls; and for individuals employed in corporate offices, banks, and department stores, removing a coat on a hot summer day was an act of major informality. When most male white-collar workers ventured outside, they usually wore a wide-brimmed fedora that looked very much like the headwear of most other men, with the exception of a few seniors who refused to relinquish their old-fashioned derbies or straw skimmers. Men's hairstyles were almost as standardized as their clothes, the main variation being a choice between maintaining the close-cropped "combat cut" that had been required in the military service or returning to the longer prewar slicked-back hair held in place by large amounts of hair tonic or cream.

These young men were now pairing off with young women who in some ways looked dramatically different from their mothers and were entering a period where comfort and formality were locked in conflict. Relatively recent women's fashions had undergone far more seismic changes than men's styles. In relatively rapid succession, the piled-up hair and long dresses of the *Titanic* era had given way to the short-skirted Flapper look of the 1920s, which in turn had morphed into the plucked eyebrows, bleached hair, and longer skirts of the depression era.

By the eve of Pearl Harbor, all of these looks seemed hopelessly old-fashioned to teenagers, college girls, and young women, and the war brought still more change. Fashion for immediate postwar females in their teens or twenties featured relatively long hair, bright red lipstick, fairly short skirts, and a seemingly infinite variety of sweaters. The practicality of pants for women in wartime factories had led to a peacetime influx of slacks, pedal pushers, and even shorts, matched with bobby sox, knee socks, saddle shoes, and loafers. While skirts or dresses topped by dressy hats and gloves were still the norm for offices, shopping, and most social occasions, home wear and informal activities were becoming increasingly casual, especially for younger women.

The preschool and elementary school children of the immediate postwar period, many of whom would later become the older siblings of the Boomers, appear in most films, advertisements, and photos to be a fusion of the prewar era and the looming 1950s. Among the most notable fashion changes for boys was a new freedom from the decades-long curse of knickers and long stockings that had separated boyhood from adolescence and produced more than a few screaming episodes of frustration as boys or their mothers tried to attach often droopy socks with tight, uncomfortable knicker pants. As prewar boys' suspenders rapidly gave way to belts, the classic prewar "newsboy" caps were being replaced by baseball caps.

Girls who would become the older sisters of the postwar generation were also caught in a bit of a fashion tug-of-war. An informal "tomboy" look of overalls, jeans, and pigtails collided with the Mary Jane dresses and bangs of the prewar era in young mothers' versions of their daughters.

The tension between past and future in American fashion was equally evident in many aspects of everyday life into which the new, postwar babies would arrive. For example, one of the first shocks that a young visitor from the twenty-first century would receive if traveling to the early postwar period would be the haze of tobacco smoke permeating almost every scene. The Boomers may have been the first generation to include substantial numbers adamantly opposed to smoking, but most of their parents and grandparents had other ideas. Nearly two of three adult males used pipes, cigars, or cigarettes, and almost two of five women were also regular smokers in the early postwar era. This was a world in which early television commercials and great numbers of full-color magazine advertisements displayed a stunningly handsome actor or a beautiful actress elegantly smoking a favorite brand of cigarette while a doctor in a white coat and stethoscope explained the ability of one brand of cigarette to keep the "T zone" free of irritation. Other doctors intoned that serious weight-watchers should "reach for a Lucky instead of a sweet." One series of magazine ads noted that in a survey of 113,597 physicians, "more doctors smoke Camels than any other brand." Even in the minority of homes where neither parent smoked, ashtrays were always readily available for the many relatives and friends who did use tobacco, thus ensuring that few Boomers would grow up in truly smoke-free homes.

The same young visitor from the twenty-first century who would be astonished at widespread tobacco use by the parents and grandparents of Boomers would find their eating habits equally cavalier. One of the most common scenes in films from the 1930s or the World War II era was a group of civilians or soldiers gathered around a fire or a foxhole dreaming of the "perfect" meal they would enjoy when the depression or the war ended. The dream fare always included steaks, bacon, a cornucopia of fried foods, and desserts, topped off with a good smoke. In an era when the real hunger of the depression and the shortages of the battlefield were still fresh memories, the prosperity of the late 1940s offered the possibility of meals where cardiovascular concerns made little difference.

The idea of a balanced diet was far from alien to the young women who would become the mothers of postwar babies. Yet this was a society in which frozen food was still a novelty, and for many families the term "icebox" continued to be a literal description of home refrigeration. Menus were still based on the seasonal availability of foods, and their ability to be "filling" continued to be emphasized. Shopping for many families was a daily excursion, and while early Boomer children would eventually be introduced to the world of gleaming supermarkets and shopping centers, a substantial part of selecting food, buying it, and preparing it was still clearly connected to earlier decades.

Along with fashion and everyday culture, another aspect of early postwar life that was caught between past and future was popular entertainment. American families living in the time immediately after World War II essentially relied on the same two major entertainment media that had dominated the preceding two decades: motion pictures and radio. A movie ticket might cost 25 to 35 cents for an adult and 10 to 15 cents for children. The first full year of peace produced the highest movie attendance in history and the release of five hundred new films. Most of them were relatively similar to their counterparts in the "golden age" of the 1930s—primarily black-and-white features of comedy, drama, romance, Westerns, or war, and dominated by a "superstar" tier of Olympian actors and actresses. Cary Grant, Errol Flynn, Gary Cooper, Humphrey Bogart, and Clark Gable commanded the most attention and money among early postwar actors; Paulette Goddard, Betty Grable, Claudette Colbert, Barbara Stanwyck, and Jane Wyman were the queens of the silver screen. A few changes could be detected when compared to the movies of the mid-1930s: the number of color films was slowly increasing, the recently ended war was still being fought on screen, and the challenge of returning to civilian life was being explored in productions like *The Best Years of Our Lives*. Some Westerns dealt with more complex social issues and a more realistic and sympathetic portrayal of Native Americans, as in *Fort Apache*.

On evenings when an excursion to the neighborhood movie theater was not planned, families gathered in their living rooms and tuned in to radio stations that supplied children's programs, classical concerts, situation comedies, mysteries, and popular music, in roughly half-hour portions. Radio was free, was accessible, and allowed varied levels of engagement, from intense concentration to background noise. It would continue to be an important if diminishing element in the awareness of the older portion of the Boomer cohort. Yet this generation was almost immediately labeled the "television generation," and there are good reasons why this identification is largely accurate.

The development of commercial television coincided almost perfectly with the beginning of the postwar surge in births. By late 1946 four television stations were on the air in the United States, with an audience of several thousand, but the possibility of geometric growth was already being discussed. A year later one magazine noted that "television is a commercial reality but not yet an art." The author explained, "Today more people want to buy sets than there are sets to buy; the television audience has soared from 53,000 sets in 1940 to one million today. After a twenty-year infancy, television is beginning to grow up. Neither the movies, nor radio, nor theater, nor any of the arts has yet developed a technique suitable to this revolutionary new medium whose possibilities, once they are recognized, will be limitless."

While the nation's 122,000 operating television sets were overwhelmingly outnumbered by 65 million radios, 2 million TVs were projected by the end of 1949. The seventeen existing television channels in late 1947 offered a variety of new experiences for viewers. American audiences were now able to witness some "breathtaking scenes. They saw and heard the United Nations and the President of the United States. As if personally in Westminster Abbey, they witnessed the marriage of a future Queen of England, televised only 29 hours after the ceremony, from newsreels flown across the ocean." Yet television also bombarded its growing audience with "some of the worst aspects of radio: implausible drama, sword swallowers, and witless chit-chat."

Fewer than ten months after this complaint appeared, another magazine explained why the new medium was changing the face of family entertainment. "Television is catching on with a speed that has amazed its own developers. It promises entertainment and advertising changes that frighten radio, movies, stage and sports industries. The 100,000 sets now in use will quadruple next year, the 38 stations will be 123 by next summer. A New York station last week announced a 7:00 A.M. to 11:00 P.M. program five days a week." Even these enormously optimistic reports could not anticipate the consequences to the new generation of children—within ten years 19 of every 20 households would own a television that would become teacher, baby-sitter, and seductress all in one.

The young men and women who would soon deal with television's siren song to their children were mainly keeping marriage license offices, obstetricians, and home builders busy in their mass transition from singlehood to parenthood. The parents of the Boomers were blazing new trails, not only in creating a surge in the birthrate but in the entire minuet that constituted courtship and marriage. Parents of Boomers had grown up in a society where marriage almost always seemed to be more acceptable than permanent bachelorhood or spinster status. A combination of the number of deaths caused by World War I and the subsequent influenza pandemic, the social dislocation of the "Roaring Twenties," and the economic depression of the thirties had left nearly one-fourth of eligible young people permanently single and many others entering less than optimal marriages in order to avoid this outcome. Then World War II and its aftermath seemed to change the rules. The global conflict shuffled the matchmaking deck in a variety of ways that created complex new relationships while sending the marriage rate soaring to new heights.

In the wake of World War II, a substantial number of postwar newlyweds had never even met before Pearl Harbor. Eligibility and attraction had been reshuffled as if by some mischievous Cupid. A young Chicago soldier who had never been south of Joliet might suddenly find himself hopelessly smitten by a Georgia girl who grew up near his base at Fort Benning. A girl from central New York, who had narrowed her potential partners to the two or three eligible boys in her town, now might find herself working at an army air corps base filled with ten thousand eligible young men and realize that a college professor from Philadelphia or a physician from Baltimore offered not only a convertible and the top dance bands at the officers' club but a whole new married adventure in a big-city suburb.

The war encouraged marriage between Northerners and Southerners, Protestants and Catholics, Americans and foreigners. The Pacific theater offered opportunities for servicemen and at least some servicewomen to discover their partners in Australia, New Zealand, the Philippines, China, and even occupied Japan. But the European theater offered far more possibilities for romantic matches. American soldiers engaged in more than a few encounters that left behind a devastated young woman or a child of mixed nationality with no legal father; but thousands of more permanent relationships developed between Yanks and European women, notably in Great Britain. One news magazine devoted a lengthy article to the arrival of one of the first "war bride" ships that sailed from England to New York after the war, carrying hundreds of foreign brides. The reunion on the docks produced a wide spectrum of emotions as some mothers with small babies introduced child and father, some men and women did not recognize their spouses, and some individually or mutually decided that the other person was not for them.

The many interregional and international relationships that did succeed produced a new generation of children who in some respects were the least parochial Americans in history. Suntanned children living in their father's Los Angeles home town found themselves slightly alien visitors among their pale cousins in their mother's birthplace of Buffalo or Rochester. Some children of war brides found themselves spending Christmas (and Boxing Day) with their British grandparents or their non-English-speaking French or Italian cousins.

As spousal preferences, employment or educational opportunities, or just a sense of adventure propelled young married couples to particular communities, a new generation of young Americans began arriving. For nearly two decades, economic disorders and war had kept birthrates at low levels. Now the combination of peace, prosperity, and a sense of new beginnings created an almost magical environment in which not just one or two children but three, four, or more became a goal for the generation of postwar parents. These young men and women were making decisions for marriage and children in a culture that largely congratulated them for their choices. Newspaper articles and magazine advertisements asked the seemingly rhetorical question, "Are Married People Happier?" and answered, "Yes, it is true that husbands and wives, particularly fathers and mothers, are happier; nationwide surveys have found that the majority of men and women agree—marriage is surely essential for happiness." While periodicals carried series on "making marriage work," or "the exciting experience of pregnancy," advertisements hinted that singles were somehow missing out.

A colorful ad for the Armstrong Cork Company in a trade magazine insisted that the addition of its new child-friendly tile floors in department stores would be the foundation of "new ideas for children's shops of the future," for catering to mothers and mothers-to-be was becoming a big business and "smart merchandizing is making it even bigger." A spacious, linoleum-floored department showed a large infant-needs area set off from the rest of the store, furnished with soft upholstered chairs to offer expectant mothers and young mothers comfort and privacy while they selected layettes. An adjacent merry-go-round display of soft toy animals "makes them accessible for impulse buying," and roomy playpens "are a comfortable, safe spot to leave a child" while registering for the next baby shower, which signaled the imminent arrival of a younger brother or sister.

There has never been a period in American history when society has not supported the production of a new generation to continue the nation's cultural heritage. But the early post–World War II era provided a particularly vigorous public and private encouragement of marriage and child-rearing seldom duplicated. Much of this stimulus emerged late in the war when, as much as the nation prayed for peace, it feared that victory and the resumption of normal life might throw the United States back into what for many Americans was the even more terrifying experience of the Great Depression.

As the war neared an end, the *New Republic* predicted, "When Demobilization Day comes we are going to suffer another Pearl Harbor perfectly foreseeable—now—a Pearl Harbor of peace, not war." Political commentator Max Lerner insisted that once the economic stimulus created by the war ended, "the unemployment rate would be one of the most serious in American history." A Gallup poll in 1944 found that half of all of those interviewed estimated that the unemployment rate would surge to between 15 and 35 percent when peace returned; the Labor Department estimated a 21 to 27 percent range. Soldiers interviewed in a government survey thought by a 2-to-1 margin that the depression would return. One of the most surprising aspects of these surveys was that their pessimistic projections were forecast during a period of unparalleled prosperity. As World War II reached its climax, unemployment in the United States dropped to 1.9 percent, the lowest in history, yet this good fortune seemed tied mainly to the demands of the conflict still raging.

The most feasible antidote to a grim future seemed to be to get women war workers back to being full-time housewives and mothers while some returning veterans filled their jobs and others returned to school to gain credentials for better jobs. The key to this complex maneuver of role switching was to convince the Rosie the Riveter generation to trade their jobs for aprons and baby bottles, thus producing employment or educational opportunity for their new husbands and new homes for the families that would hopefully follow. The main engines for this social revolution proved to be an innocuous-sounding piece of legislation called the Servicemen's Readjustment Act and an unpretentiously titled book, *Baby and Child Care*, by Benjamin Spock, M.D.

Each of these documents empowered young couples to believe they could create households and families surpassing any past generation in comfort, caring, and security for their children.

The Servicemen's Readjustment Act was passed in September 1944 and was quickly shortened for everyday use to the "G.I. Bill." More than 15 million servicemen and women were eligible for educational benefits under the bill, including full tuition to an educational institution of the veteran's choice, a $35 monthly stipend for single students, $90 a month for married veterans, and up to $120 a month for students with children.

This sliding scale influenced the creation of postwar families by prompting a rearrangement of the traditional school, marriage, family continuum. Now many marriages and births would occur parallel to college study. Hundreds of postwar campuses featured married and family housing, ranging from surplus Quonset huts and converted military barracks to more comfortable apartment houses. Mostly male veterans would emerge each morning from these "Vetsvilles" or "Fertile Acres" to confront Philosophy or Business Law while their young wives dealt with the challenge of child-rearing on the cheap. At the University of Minnesota's Veterans Village by 1948 there were 936 new babies and even more toddlers. The Village had a twelve-member board of aldermen made up of eleven young mothers and only one man. It decreed that any adult automatically became the temporary guardian of an unsupervised child, and initiated the right to spank any child who attempted to cross a dangerous street alone. Group shopping and baby-sitting were promoted, and the limited supply of home appliances was commonly shared by all.

Married students at Stanford University: the G.I. Bill not only strained classroom facilities in postwar colleges but also created a new, parallel collegiate culture in which fraternity parties gave way to baby-sitting, trips to the playground, and shopping excursions. *(Time & Life Pictures/Getty Images)*

As of April 1947, of 2,000 married veterans at the University of Wisconsin in Madison, 800 already had new babies, and 288 others had wives in first pregnancies. The university persuaded the state's Public Housing Authority to send in hundreds of prefab buildings that had been used for war workers, which now clustered around a cooperative grocery store, a bowling alley, and a community recreation center.

The millions of married veterans and their spouses, who largely abandoned fried chicken for chicken soup and set up housekeeping in "homes" that had only recently served military purposes, faced a demanding experience that drove many young men and women to the limits of their endurance. Veterans attempted to study amid the din of screaming babies and noisy toddlers, not helped by paper-thin walls, while their wives set up housekeeping with few conveniences or appliances. Yet it seems likely that a substantial number of these young couples saw their young children as a symbol of their independence from older relatives and older lifestyles and believed they had embarked on a marvelous adventure in this new "Atomic Age."

One of the developments that made this great new adventure more manageable for young married couples, whether they lived in Fertile Acres or in more traditional housing, was the publication in 1946 of Dr. Benjamin Spock's *Baby and Child Care*, a paperback book that sold for 35 cents and was designed specifically for anxious young postwar parents. The book would go on to sell 30 million copies in 29 languages before the last Boomer was born, becoming the best-selling new title ever published in the United States to that time. Young mothers, from former war workers to future first lady Jacqueline Kennedy, were effusive in their praise of Dr. Spock's reassuring, nonjudgmental approach, which explained that a simple combination of relaxation, persistence, and, above all, a sense of humor would solve most baby care issues, and that trust in one's innate maternal and paternal instincts was an excellent first step in the parenting experience.

The book included space for birth statistics, records of checkups, parent questions for the doctor, and an infant's height and weight chart, along with advice that parents should enjoy their babies yet accept that some level of frustration was normal in all parenting activities. Spock admitted that "Children keep parents from parties, trips, theaters, meetings, games and friends: The fact that you prefer children and wouldn't trade places with a childless couple for

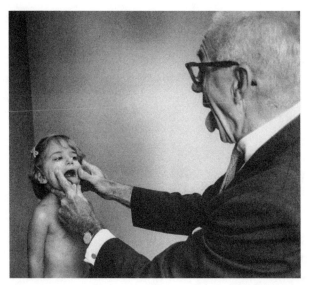

Dr. Benjamin Spock, above, emphasized a commonsense, relaxed approach to postwar child-rearing. His book on baby and child care became one of the best-selling books of modern times. *(Time & Life Pictures/Getty Images)*

anything doesn't alter the fact that you still miss your freedom." Yet the rewards from this lifestyle were almost limitless, according to Spock, for compared with "this creation, this visible immortality, pride in other worldly accomplishments is usually weak in comparison." On the other hand, if sacrifice was healthy, the martyrdom of needless self-sacrifice was counterproductive: "parents will become so preoccupied and tense that they're no fun for outsiders or for each other."

Benjamin Spock had the great good fortune to be accepted as authoritative and wise in a generally upbeat, pragmatic culture of young parenthood. His book gave young men and women permission to expand the traditional boundaries of parental involvement with and even indulgence in their children's lives. These new parents were more willing to buy toys, less willing to use corporal punishment, and more open to friendship with their children than their own parents had been. New parenting now included playgroups, incentives for good behavior, and even children's opinions in the forging of family decisions, from meals to vacations. New mothers were less often drill sergeants and more often counselors and advisers. New fathers were more involved and less forbidding.

When these young parents had a rare moment to consider their role in the chain of generations of mothers and fathers, they often sensed a certain uniqueness in their experience. First, it gradually became evident that more of them were having children, and the numbers of children were larger in an American society that until recently had seemed to be moving toward fewer and later marriages, and fewer children. Second, they were being assured in books, films, and political speeches that their experience was vital to the nation's welfare and future prosperity. Third, they were aware that demographic and technological changes were rapidly redefining the kind of life they would live and where they would live it. If Benjamin Spock opened a new frontier in the experience of parenting, a fast-talking, chain-smoking former naval construction engineer opened a new portal on the kind of home life where many of them would raise these new families. William Levitt's transformation of a vast expanse of Long Island potato fields into a planned, child-friendly suburban community would inaugurate a new family experience for the Baby Boomers and their young parents.

\\\|//
2

HOME AND FAMILY IN
EARLY POSTWAR AMERICA

ONE OF THE MOST endearing films of the immediate postwar era gained much of its box-office popularity by recounting a modern fairy tale in which the prize is not a throne or riches but a "castle" in a new form of community that would come to define a newly emerging American lifestyle. *Miracle on 34th Street* is a story of the hopes and dreams of a little girl, played by Natalie Wood, living in a Manhattan apartment with her single mother, a Macy's employee played by Maureen O'Hara. Cautioned by her mother to be skeptical of belief in Santa Claus, the little girl is coaxed into revealing her one true wish by a department store Santa who calls himself Kris Kringle. Dolls, toys, and cycles hold little interest for a girl who dreams of escaping the restrictions of apartment life for a new home in the suburbs, preferably with a new father who will complete a traditional family. When Kringle (Edmund Gwenn) is fired as Macy's Santa and nearly committed to a mental hospital, a young bachelor lawyer played by John Payne choreographs a brilliant defense that acquits his client and sparks the beginning of a romantic interest with the single mother. As mother, daughter, and bachelor drive home from a suburban Christmas morning celebration, Natalie Wood orders Payne to stop the car and runs across a lawn into her "dream home," which is empty and for sale. Payne and O'Hara run after her and discover their love for each other in an empty living room that holds only the cane used by Kris Kringle. The "miracle" is an escape from Thirty-fourth Street and a new beginning in a new family and a suburban home.

While few early postwar families could match the miraculous nature of this transition from urban crowding to a spacious suburban home, the film struck a major chord in the desire for young parents to establish themselves in a new frontier of lawns, picture windows, and barbeque pits—a lifestyle that seemed especially congenial to growing families of the new Baby Boom.

Postwar suburban development had its antecedents in the rise of earlier "bedroom communities" adjacent to large cities. Earlier in the twentieth century, the emergence of railroads, trolley cars, and other forms of public transportation had allowed workers in New York, Philadelphia, Chicago, and other cities to commute from suburban homes to downtown jobs. The depression and World War II, however, had brought suburban home construction nearly to a halt. Even in a more positive economic environment, early suburbs had often been tethered to rail lines, and huge swaths of land beyond the range of public transportation remained underutilized. Then, just as the G.I. Bill expanded veterans' educational frontiers with its tuition grants and subsidies, it also encouraged new housing frontiers through its mortgage benefits.

One of the major barriers to home ownership in pre–
World War II America was the size of the down payment.
The Servicemen's Readjustment Act largely changed the
rules by allowing a number of circumstances where the government would essentially guarantee the mortgage loan and
encourage a policy of no down payment. The first entrepreneur who fully appreciated the impact of this provision was
William Levitt, a New Yorker who had spent his wartime
service managing the mass construction of buildings for the
U.S. Navy.

Soon after his discharge, the forty-three-year-old veteran,
described as a "cocky, rambunctious hustler with the hoarse
voice of a three-pack-a-day smoker," bought twelve hundred
acres of potato farmland near Hicksville, on Long Island
about twenty miles outside of New York City. He turned his
military organizational abilities into a construction campaign designed to entice young buyers into believing they
could secure a part of the new American dream of home
ownership in the pristine world of suburbia. From dawn
to dusk in the muddy fields of a rising community called
Levittown, the ground would shake as a convoy of tractors
rumbled like charging squadrons of Sherman tanks. Every
hundred feet they would dump identical bundles of lumber,
pipe, boards, shingles, and copper tubing, all so neatly pack-
aged they resembled enormous loaves of bread dropped by
a bakery operated by giants. Then other massive machines
fitted with a seemingly endless chain of buckets dug into the
earth to form a trench around a twenty-five-by-thirty-two-
foot rectangle. As men and machines engaged in a carefully
coordinated operation, a new house would emerge largely
complete every fifteen minutes until by July 1950 more than
eleven thousand nearly identical homes sprawled across the

The three original Levittown communities in New York, New Jersey, and Pennsylvania, above, symbolized the emergence of modern suburban lifestyles.
By the sixties some Boomers would criticize their childhood homes as "ticky-
tacky boxes." *(Time & Life Pictures/Getty Images)*

fields, with parallel Levittowns rising in Pennsylvania and
New Jersey.

A sale price of $7,990 bought mostly young couples a
new home that, even if it would never be mistaken for a
castle, offered a phenomenally child-friendly environment
in which to raise a rapidly expanding family. Each home
featured a picture window fronting a twelve-by-fifteen-foot
living room, a bathroom, a kitchen, two bedrooms, and an
"expansion attic," which could and usually was converted
to two more bedrooms and an additional bath. Each house
was equipped with a refrigerator, stove, washing machine,
fireplace, and built-in seven-inch television.

While young couples fired barbeque grills and their children raced tricycles and used their skate keys, most Americans who were either single or over thirty-five initially stayed well clear of the planned-community experience. Levittown and its hundreds of nationwide clones were worlds teeming with children and baby carriages but largely devoid of nightclubs and taverns. The first Levittown was peppered with huge new shopping centers, surrounded by enormous parking lots easily accessible from connecting roads. More than a hundred miles of winding streets and sidewalks teemed with vehicles partial to children, from station wagons to kiddy carts. If myriad descriptions were accurate, young mothers pushed strollers, held toddlers' hands, dodged tricycles, and swapped recipes in the morning until an eerie silence descended on most of the community around noon. The next two hours were a mutually refreshing respite as children napped and mothers slumped into chairs or caught up on other chores. As late as 1950, only 10 percent of the children of Levittown were over seven years of age, encouraging one mother to explain that "Everyone is so young that sometimes it's hard to remember to get along with older people." The absence of an older adult presence contrasted with a seemingly limitless array of parks, playgrounds, baseball diamonds, swimming pools, and kiddie pools that seemed to cater to every whim, as long as it was a young whim.

Levittown was only the first of thousands of suburban "subdivisions" that would eventually define much of America's postwar lifestyle and become one of the iconic images of film, television, and literature. If suburbia could sometimes be made into a fantasy—either dreamlike or nightmarish, depending on the narrator's outlook—it was also the home of a substantial portion of the Boomer generation. Still, many postwar children grew up in places where their parents, grandparents, and great-grandparents had spent their respective childhoods, and these locales continued to strike an important chord in the song of American culture. Children grew up in the rural farmland depicted on television programs such as *Lassie* and *The Real McCoys*; others experienced a small-town childhood, still a major topic of Normal Rockwell's iconic artwork; many Boomers resided in large cities, as reflected in TV's *Make Room for Daddy*. This author grew up in an "inner ring" suburb of Philadelphia, which had largely developed in the 1920s and 1930s. There stone Tudor singles mingled with brick twins and row houses, corner delicatessens, taprooms, and trolley cars, which hinted at an urban lifestyle while coexisting with the swimming pools, Little League fields, and barbeque grills that defined postwar suburban living. All of these environments featured many young couples with large numbers of children but also included senior citizens, single people, and childless couples, which made them appear slightly less Baby Boomer centered. Yet, in the postwar era, newer suburbs dominated by young couples and children often defined the Boomer experience in films, literature, and television. Since this suburban lifestyle offers both the distinctiveness of a new childhood experience and many elements of the more general experience of all Boomers, Levittown and its counterparts make a good introduction to the postwar home and family.

The physical makeup of a Boomer-era childhood home reflected the design of three prominent suburban models: colonial, ranch, and split-level. Colonials were, at first glance, the closest approximation to the "Victorian" homes

The most popular postwar suburban home model was the ranch house. The single-floor layout eliminated the tedium of stair climbing, but many families found more togetherness than they wanted with bedrooms in close proximity to living rooms. *(Times & Life Pictures/Getty Images)*

characteristic of much of the Northeast and Midwest and popular in most other sections of the country since the turn of the century. These are the homes most often seen in 1950s and 1960s family situation comedies and films, and featured the most traditional living arrangements. A colonial had two full stories with living room, kitchen, and dining room on the ground floor, bedrooms and bathrooms on the second floor, and often a basement and/or an attic. Unlike their Victorian predecessors, however, colonials largely dispensed with front parlors, front porches, and pantries, substituting powder rooms, dens, and rear decks. This configuration provided the advantage of relatively large kitchens that could also accommodate a table for meals, less intrusive noise for children sleeping upstairs, and the possibility of relatively generous storage space. The two major drawbacks of colonials were that they tended to be more expensive than other models, and the stairs could become extremely annoying when having to carry toddlers or wash baskets.

The ranch was probably the most popular home model for the entire Baby Boom childhood period. Ranches tended to be rather sprawling homes with virtually all the living space concentrated on one floor. These houses looked very contemporary, eliminated most stair climbing, and, like the colonials, might include a basement or an attic that could offer more room as families grew. This living arrangement was less frequently depicted on film and television but was the most common new housing in American suburbs.

The third home model was generally a compromise between colonial and ranch—usually, but not always, designated a split-level. This style offered three or even four floors, divided by stairs that were roughly half the extent of steps in traditional two-story homes. In most cases, upper levels featured bedrooms; middle levels had kitchens, dining rooms, and living rooms; and lower levels included laundry rooms, garage access, powder rooms, and the most innovative of postwar suburbia, a "family room" or "recreation room" that often included a television, record-player system, a new "recliner" chair or two, and perhaps a fireplace, pool table, or Ping-Pong table. In many homes this room might become a gathering place for younger members of the family while the living room was used by adults or reserved for relatively formal occasions.

Most of the new ranches and at least some of the colonials and split-levels had a feature that illustrated the downside of postwar tract housing. Many 1950s and 1960s homes were not only considerably smaller than their twenty-first-century counterparts, they were also more cramped and shoddily constructed than models built several decades earlier. Traditional attics and basements had become less than standard features on "contemporary" homes, creating a never-ending storage crisis. Bulky children's items such as tricycles, bicycles, and strollers vied with lawn mowers, grills, and gardening equipment in crawl spaces, garages, and driveways. Even that icon of suburban upward mobility, the two-car garage, frequently became the no-car garage, containing every wheeled object except an automobile.

The interior of a new Boomer-era home was often equally cramped. Cost-cutting imperatives reduced halls to a claustrophobic width of thirty-six inches, which turned passage from one room to another into a complex maneuver when two family members met along the route. Many new kitchens had space for a counter and stools, but the absence of a traditional table often turned breakfast into a stand-up meal on the go. The combination of thin walls and one-floor design in a ranch home often made adult television viewing in the living room a major sleep impediment for younger children, who might have to put pillows over their ears to reduce laugh tracks and commercial noise. One of many *Life* articles on the realities of suburban living implied that behind the façade of cozy ranches were frayed nerves and petty arguments caused by close quarters and unstored toys.

Whatever the merits or defects of postwar homes, they became the setting for a frenetic social drama centered on new parents and their burgeoning families. While there was no "ideal" or "typical" Boomer family, some general patterns are noticeable. First, the average marriage age for young men and women was gradually falling until in 1957 it reached 21.5 years for males and 19.5 for females. This meant that a large percentage of girls were becoming engaged late in high school or very early in college. Newspaper wedding announcements featured great numbers of teenage brides and only marginally more mature grooms. Second, these young newlyweds started their families quickly, which in turn pushed the average family size toward four children. By the mid-1950s more families had six children than had one child, while childless couples seemed relegated to peripheral status in family dynamics. The cast of characters in these ongoing family dramas also included fewer non-nuclear family members as the number of grandparents, aunts, uncles, and cousins living full time in the same family home as mother, father, and children dropped substantially.

The family-life dramas that engaged young Americans across the continent showed considerable continuity with past counterparts but contained enough unique aspects to promote interest decades later. A peek into a representative 1950s home would often reveal an amazingly young, rather formally dressed mother barely out of her teens, organizing a household of several children and deputizing the slightly older ones to take some responsibility for their younger siblings while she cleaned, shopped, and cooked. In this occasionally magic and frequently hectic environment, older children became confidants to their young mothers as they formed a special bond based on their partial responsibility for the great enterprise of "family life."

While spanking and screaming at children had not disappeared from parents' corrective repertoire, the strict environment of earlier decades had mellowed considerably as many mothers exhibited the patience, grace, and intelligence of the well-known TV mothers—a June Cleaver, a Donna Reed, or a Harriet Nelson—while often interacting with far more children than their television counterparts.

Gender roles also seemed to be gradually softening as the postwar family structure crystallized. Far more postwar women drove automobiles than their mothers had, both through the necessity of a car-oriented suburban culture and a sense of empowerment that driving was not exclusively a male prerogative. In those suburbs with access to public transportation, the wife often logged more driving time than the commuter train–dependent father, who was now relegated to weekend and vacation driving in a vehicle that had tacitly become "mom's car." As driving errands now shifted to more of a female role, the rise of the "barbeque" culture turned more than a few men into amateur cooks. Contrary to myths that hapless 1950s males found heating a frozen TV dinner daunting, this era turned much of the outdoor cooking experience into a male domain. From backyard grills to picnic fireplaces, young fathers, with or without "World's Greatest Chef" hats, became iconic figures of the period and often passed their skills to their sons. The gradual shift to more night and weekend hours, from pediatricians' offices to supermarkets, also contributed to a softening of gender roles as doctors' visits and shopping excursions more frequently engaged both husband and wife far more than the strict weekday hours of prewar shopping and services.

Gender roles among children were also changing, more than is apparent from looking merely at the doctor/nurse divide in medically oriented toys. The black toy doctor bag did have stern-looking glasses, absent from the white nurse bag, and included more active diagnostic instruments and fewer bandages. But the distinction between "cowboys" and "cowgirls" was much smaller, as girls were "allowed" to have guns, holsters, hats, and boots, much the same as boys.

Perhaps the most flexible gender relationships occurred as older children were often designated junior parents in the crowded households of the times. Many boys changed younger siblings' diapers, took them for walks in strollers, and rode their bikes to the store with a grocery list from their mothers. Girls helped move heavy furniture, showed their little brothers how to play basketball, and helped their mothers wash and polish the car. Various levels of baby-sitting experience often depended more on age than on gender; few parents would hire an outside baby-sitter to watch younger children if there was a twelve-year-old son in the house, and at least some boys expanded their baby-sitting to include neighbors' kids, just as girls took on newspaper deliveries in some communities.

Much of the image of American society from the late 1940s to the early 1960s is based on the concept of a comfortable but rather conservative lifestyle with relatively little questioning of the status quo. Yet investigation of contemporary sources reveals that discussions about optimal methods of parenting and adult-child relations were noticeable in almost every medium, and young couples were convinced and delighted that they were entering a new frontier of family relationships. In fact, period discussions about the 1950s equivalents of "soccer moms," "helicopter parents," and "tweeners" culture appear quite modern in tone. Yet, along with these recognizable concerns there are strong suggestions that the fifteen to twenty years following World War II were indeed "Happy Days" for both parents and their children.

Most important, this period represents one of the high points of family stability in the entire American experience. Earlier in the century, the high mortality of parents from epidemics, work-related accidents, and childbirth complications produced a strong possibility that childhood would be marred by orphanage residence, unpleasant stepparents, difficult stepsiblings, or placement with less than welcoming aunts, uncles, or cousins. Later in the century, after the Boomer age, skyrocketing divorce rates and a sharp rise in out-of-wedlock births created a parallel world of uncertainty and lack of affection for children. Yet for a relatively brief period, the optimistic portrayal of childhood and family experience in the media and literature of postwar America did reflect reality. Children lived in a world of stable and seemingly happy marriages where divorce seemed to be a feature primarily of the Hollywood acting community, and fatalities from work accidents, disease, and childbirth were substantially reduced. The only family distress that was significantly more likely in the early postwar period than in the twenty-first century was the far higher incidence of childhood disease. At best, most children and their frazzled parents lived through bouts of measles, chickenpox, and mumps, which, if seldom fatal, were rather serious illnesses requiring considerable bed rest and intense parental care. The majority of early Boomer children also experienced a painful trip to the hospital as pediatricians seemed obsessed about the health implications of swollen tonsils. Relatively few children escaped a tonsillectomy, whose pain and hospitalization were offset by the dubious promise of "all the ice cream you can eat" after the operation. But by far the most terrifying shadow hovering over any family was infantile paralysis, the polio that had crippled the recently deceased president and spurred the annual March of Dimes campaigns. The crippling or death of tens of thousands of Boomer children was quite possibly the single greatest calamity in postwar households until Dr. Jonas Salk joined Benjamin Spock in the pantheon of parental heroes when he perfected the first successful polio immunization vaccine in 1955.

The benign influence of relatively high levels of family stability was paired with relaxed discipline and heightened parental involvement that made the period a nostalgic era for children. American mothers of the period often appear as confident, friendly, caring young women who drove children to shopping centers, splashed them in a backyard pool, and served milk and cookies to a circle of avid television viewers. Fathers emerge as relaxed, strong, involved figures who were less likely to spend the evening with "the boys" in a local tavern or bowling alley and were now finding their stride as Little League coaches and scout leaders. But if the specter of childhood disease was the dark cloud threatening an otherwise stable family structure, excessive parental involvement now emerged as a less positive side of the "child-friendly" attitude of the period.

A 1958 article by Robert Paul Smith, a rising expert on parent-child relations, coined the mildly disturbing term "Big Brother Parents," which hinted at an almost Orwellian control of childhood activities. Smith lamented the rise of "a well-intentioned horde of interfering parents who give their kids no chance to have fun by themselves." In an almost eerie preview of twenty-first-century issues, the author insisted, "The way you play soccer now is you bring home from school a mimeographed schedule for the Saturday morning leagues. The schedule is arranged by a mathematical process of permutation that would take six mathematicians to figure out. Parents are now playing someone else's game. All the parents who cannot refrain from interfering in the wonderful world of a child have invented a whole new modern posture—child watching." Smith empathized with a young mother who complained that when her daughter was "initiated" in the Brownies, all the mothers had to be admitted too, a ceremony that concluded with an almost comic scene of the mothers standing in a line and reciting the Brownie oath. Similar articles reported that while young parents were often delighted that their children liked spending time playing under adult supervision, many of the youngsters were embarrassed when the parents made spectacles of themselves as Little League umpires or replaced their daughters when going door-to-door to sell Girl Scout cookies. A major question of the time was whether parents wanted their children to be more grown up, or whether parents wanted to be more like their kids.

At first glance the home setting for young Boomer children would look rather contemporary to a twenty-first-century observer. The house would be bright, airy, and well lit, the kitchen appliances would appear modern, and the youthful noise would be familiar. On closer inspection, substantial differences would begin to appear. In summer, the cool, quiet hum of central air-conditioning systems would give way to steamy warmth, only slightly moderated by noisy electric fans dotted around the house. Before the very end of the 1950s, entertainment and communication devices would most likely be limited to one black-and-white television with a twelve- to twenty-one-inch screen; a floor- or table-model radio in the living room; one or two black, dial telephones, one located in the kitchen, living room, or entrance hall with a possible second in the parents' bedroom; and a "hi-fi" record player stocked with 33⅓ rpm albums.

A glance at children's bedrooms would reveal two important differences from the twenty-first century. Depending on the age of the occupants, the bedrooms would include toy chests; posters of movies, comic-book heroes, or music celebrities; sports pennants and photos; and similar decorations. Few electronic devices could be found, and human child voices would be much more common than any other sound. Some fortunate children of the late 1950s might have their families' old twelve-inch television sets if a new twenty-one-inch model had been purchased; some children would have a small plastic clock radio on a nightstand. Preteens might have a small record player capable of playing a stack of the new 45 rpm "singles" that emerged with the birth of rock music. A tiny number of relatively affluent preteens or early teenagers, especially girls, might have their own phones, but this was a coveted possession seen much more often on television or in films than in real bedrooms.

A second important difference, compared to the twenty-first century, was the bedroom with two or even three beds. The growing number of bedrooms in new home styles never kept pace with the increase in family size of the period, and the result was a premium on shared sleeping space. Most new homes featured three bedrooms, and since a fairly typical Boomer-era family had three to five children, bedroom sharing was almost inevitable. Most children's bedrooms featured either two twin beds or a bunk-bed configuration, but a single twin bed and a double bunk were also common in families with five or more children or families with four kids with a 3-to-1 gender ratio. Given space limitations, families might allow mixed accommodations among young children, but this was usually a temporary stopgap before a move or home expansion.

A closer examination of other rooms in a Boomer household would reveal other technological limitations that often affected the childhood experience. A modern 1950s kitchen included a refrigerator and stove, sometimes in matching colors, and a sink that often came with a spray hose attachment. Microwave ovens were still primarily a figment of science fiction, and automatic dishwashers would be uncommon for another decade. The "TV dinner" was now available and heavily advertised but in fact was viewed largely as a backup or emergency alternative; few housewives would dream of serving them regularly. This level of technology had relieved much of the drudgery of a half-century earlier, but in food preparation and after-meal cleanup the mother could assume that she would receive at least some family help. A laundry room or basement would reveal the same mixed technology. Most homes now had an electric washing machine; relatively few still featured the external hand-operated wringer. But automatic gas or electric dryers were still a novelty until well into the 1960s, and wash day featured a backyard filled with intricate clotheslines with an array of clothes, towels, and sheets flapping in the breeze like colorful sails. Doing the wash also called for children's help, and very few Boomer kids reached adulthood without knowing how to use clothespins or how heavy a basket of wet wash might be.

Thus even a cursory tour of an average Boomer's childhood home would reveal three somewhat different realities compared to a twenty-first-century experience. First, technology was still relatively limited; second, privacy was very limited; and third, the concept of children's chores was still an important part of family life. The many Boomer childhood ideas about cooperation, boredom, fun, and adult authority might be different from those of their children and grandchildren.

The children of this era fought over viewing preferences on the single television set, played Monopoly or Clue on the living-room floor with brothers, sisters, and friends, screamed that an obnoxious sibling had "cooties," and helped one another put on snow boots that seemed to feature an infinite number of finicky buckles. A world of relatively large families and tighter household budgets guaranteed numerous variations on the theme of sharing, ranging from cutting jelly doughnuts in half to group ownership of some toys. Almost every household activity became an exercise in negotiating or bartering, yet these actions were so common that few children consciously thought about them.

A shared bedroom made privacy a luxury, and the limited capacity of hot-water heaters virtually guaranteed that a warm shower could turn frigid in the rush for the school bus. Yet there were always plenty of available players for Scrabble or Crazy Eights, and older brothers and sisters were more often protective and caring than obnoxious and bossy. This meant that unless a child was the oldest in the family, when Boomer kids made their first treks to school, they would not be alone. This comfort, however, was scarcely reassuring to the harried principals and teachers who watched a tidal wave of youngsters surge into their already bulging institutions. While Boomer homes might be crowded, it was the jammed classrooms that were now gaining national attention.

\\\ll//

3

SCHOOL DAZE:
FROM SPLIT SHIFTS TO SPUTNIK

BENJAMIN SPOCK'S cheerful suggestions on baby and child care encouraged many young parents to believe they could somehow meet the challenges of rearing multiple children. But in school district offices across the country, the surging birthrate was prompting a crisis atmosphere that would dominate educational policies for almost two decades. Unlike parents, obstetricians, and pediatricians, most school officials and teachers did not have to deal with the impact of the Baby Boom from the time of its inception in January 1946. It would be early in the next decade before the first cohort of Boomers reached school. On a series of bright, late-summer days in 1952, however, the Boomers and the American school system were introduced to each other in the educational equivalent of the Normandy invasion.

A year earlier, school personnel had received a preview of coming attractions when a mixture of the youngest war babies and the oldest Boomers had crowded schools designed largely for low prewar birthrates. Now, in 1952, the first class made up entirely of Boomers, the future high school class of 1964 and the college class of 1968, pushed public school attendance over the 34 million mark amid projections that even this staggering number would increase by an additional 50 percent by the end of the fifties. (In 1940 school attendance had been 25.4 million.) Unlike an enemy sneak attack or a natural disaster, the initial surge of children into first grade occurred with plenty of advance warning. But the heroic responses of a nation at war had perhaps worn thin in peacetime as half-measures, wishful thinking, and competing educational demands produced an educational crisis that at times threatened to spin out of control. For example, in the early 1950s the percentage of teenagers remaining in high school until graduation was soaring just as the Boomers hit the lower grades, forcing superintendents to create stopgap measures at opposite ends of the educational ladder. Semi-rural areas that had made do with a single consolidated school were now burgeoning suburbs requiring six new elementary schools at the same time. Low prewar birthrates had produced a meager pool of new teachers—just as the need for their services exploded.

As late summer 1952 turned to autumn, a nation concerned with Soviet spy rings, a new addition to Lucy and Ricky's television family, and the stretch drive of the baseball season would find it difficult to miss the media attention to the emerging crisis of overcrowding in the schools. Magazines, newspapers, and television news began running pictures of cute young children doubling up two to a desk, sharing textbooks, and jamming lunchrooms. Harried superintendents and principals showed visitors classrooms bulging with forty or fifty pupils, and predicted even higher numbers to come. Extensive parochial school systems in Northeastern and Midwestern cities dispatched nuns from retirement homes and shortened training periods for young novice sisters to cover gaps in schools that often exceeded sixty students per classroom.

While parents and school officials fretted over this classroom overcrowding, more than a few Boomer children saw the experience as a memorable adventure. Teachers might see row upon row of cherubic faces that created multiple opportunities for calling a pupil by the wrong name, but the children took the situation in stride. A girl alternately called Joan, Jean, or Jane, or a boy addressed as John, Joseph, or Jerry, realized that adult teachers were not all-knowing and teased one another with their "alternate" names, which brought laughter all around. Some Boomers adopted a sort of perverse pride in the size of their class enrollments, especially when the youngest students eyed the much smaller class sizes in the upper grades. The older kids might be bigger and stronger, but the Boomers had sheer numbers on their side. Some level of unique group identity may have been developing well before most of this generation had any idea what the term meant.

Despite children's lack of concern, adults saw these school problems as a major issue for the nation's future. An extensive editorial essay in the October 1952 *Life* magazine focused on overcrowding in one New York City school. Max Francke, the principal of a school with 2,011 students in a building with a capacity of 1,470, was engaged in an endless game of musical chairs with his Boomer kindergarten and first-grade pupils. "My teachers are tired, the crowding is getting them down, there are so many five and six year olds, and they will move up through the higher grades next year."

All students at the school were required to wear paper name and address tags while mothers were given a printed timetable to let them know when the teachers would bring their children to the school door. Francke noted that the enrollment of 245 in the second grade was dwarfed by the 430 first-graders who overwhelmed school capacity. "Over 500 children are getting five hours less class work than the law requires, and they confuse parents by entering and leaving at odd hours" in the first stage of a split-shift configuration. One mother who had two children in different shifts complained, "For years I've been looking forward to getting both kids from under my feet at the same time. Now that isn't happening."

As traditional school buildings were engulfed by the surging enrollment, officials opened classrooms in town halls, firehouses, and church basements. A few desperate districts turned school buses into classrooms between their pickups and deliveries. The Linda Mar housing estate, fifteen miles east of San Francisco, rented eleven of its homes as schools for $850 a month. A Long Island developer demonstrated his civic spirit by paying construction crews to work overtime and weekends to prepare ten houses as classrooms in time for the post–Labor Day surge of new pupils. As classes met, tractors were still smoothing dirt in front yards. Partitions were temporarily left out of construction in order to provide classrooms with enough space to hold the swelling student population. The pastor of a suburban Philadelphia Catholic parish purchased a house across the street from the school, placed the first-graders in the building, and received township provision for an all-day crossing guard to shepherd six-year-olds across the street to use the main building's lavatories.

The national shortage of classrooms, which reached 370,000 by 1953, was matched by a burgeoning teacher deficit which one educational writer attributed to "matrimony, maternity and more money elsewhere." During the ensuing decade, nearly 200,000 teaching appointments would be left unfilled at the close of each academic year, yet the most sensible solution to attract new people to the profession— substantial pay raises—always seemed to be the last resort. West Hartford, Connecticut, which counted 109 unfilled teaching positions in a staff of 400, encouraged new applicants with a community square dance, help in finding housing, a Rotary Club welcome luncheon, and gifts to anyone who signed a contract. The PTA pooled its resources to locate families willing to take in teachers as temporary boarders at little or no rent. On a national level, magazine advertisements and television public service programs portrayed teachers as key personnel in the expansion of the American economy and the defense of liberty. Placed among color photos of new refrigerators and ranges, the Norge Corporation announced that "American elementary schools are now short 120,700 teachers—this means overcrowded classes, half days, and other shortcomings. Write for practical information that you can do as a concerned citizen."

Journals specializing in educational affairs devoted entire issues to the Boomer tidal wave. In "Our Children Are Still Being Cheated" in its October 1953 issue, the *Elementary School Journal* warned that worse problems were on the way as "the number of children will increase another 1.6 million this year, and by 1960, there will be 10 million more students than today." School districts were building an additional 97,000 classrooms, but even that campaign would leave 60 percent of all classes overcrowded, with 20 percent of schools unable to meet even minimal fire safety requirements.

The *Journal* pointed out that mere stabilization of class sizes at current overcrowded levels would require 425,000 new classrooms by the end of the 1950s while university teacher training programs had produced only 46,000 new elementary teachers for the 118,000 additional positions that school districts had created. These equations meant that the best-case scenario for the immediate future was an average class size of 45 children, with even larger classes if the teacher gap continued to worsen.

The surge of new students consigned large numbers of children to a learning environment of dilapidated classrooms manned by overtaxed teachers. Yet two compensating factors emerged to make the school experience of the 1950s and 1960s much less grim than initially feared. First, a massive school construction effort, even if plagued by shortfalls, offered the opportunity for a relatively large number of Boomers to attend schools that were much more modern and cheerful than those from their parents' childhoods. Burgeoning suburban communities constructed gleaming, airy, attractive schools with glass walls, offering a vista of pleasant grounds. Banks of new fluorescent lights brightly illuminated classrooms on the most dismal winter days, and movable desks replaced the regimented rows bolted to the floor. New schools often featured a single-floor format where classrooms were interspersed with spacious arcades and growing numbers of special-activity rooms. School architects found themselves free to experiment with dramatic innovations that spelled the end of the last vestiges of the "little red schoolhouse."

A second potential benefit of the Boomer surge was a greater receptiveness toward the use of new technology to at least partially counteract the ongoing teacher shortage. Tape recorders, portable record players, transistor radios, and enhanced filmstrips offered significant opportunities to create new learning environments. The most frequently discussed new educational technology was the emergence of television as an increasingly dominant medium. As families flocked to buy televisions that would penetrate the majority of American households by 1954, a national debate erupted over the role of the instrument in the learning process.

One national news weekly provoked substantial public response to an article titled "The 21-inch Classroom," which suggested that "If it lives up to its promise, television will revolutionize teaching as nothing else since the American public school was established. Television may alleviate the critical teacher shortage, as television in both closed-circuit and over-the-air educational and commercial stations emerge. Despite the possible dangers in television, the results are so encouraging that the number of schools using it is doubling every year, and the time they allot to TV instruction is rising rapidly." One example cited was the Hagerstown, Maryland, school district, which developed a closed-circuit system. By 1957 it was providing all children from first to twelfth grades with televised lessons from a central studio in which a teacher could reach seventeen hundred students at once.

Much of the funding for experiments in instructional television was provided by major Ford Foundation grants. Some parents believed their children were already getting too much television at home, and more than a few suspected that the new medium might someday replace conventional teachers altogether. Yet in an environment where the teacher shortage was projected to reach 500,000 by 1965, televised instruction gained increasing legitimacy.

As a growing number of educators envisioned a not too distant future when "a special device will enable pupils to interact with the televised teacher hundreds of miles away,"

While many parents' groups and child psychologists warned of the dire consequences of television's effects on Boomer children, much of the educational establishment welcomed the video revolution as a means to broaden pupil horizons and help overstretched teachers and administrators. *(Bettmann/ CORBIS)*

most 1950s children spent their school day learning from textbooks that were not greatly different from the lessons their parents had received. The centerpiece of instruction at the elementary level was still literacy teaching, and in many cases this meant an encounter with a "typical American family" featuring Dick and Jane, their toddler sister Sally, Spot the dog, Puff the cat, a pipe-smoking father, and a pretty, well-organized mother. Short repetitive sentences, such as, "See Spot. See Spot run. Run Spot Run," interspersed with colorful pictures of family activities and interaction, began the great adventure of reading in an era when the printed word had far less competition for attention that it would in the twenty-first century.

The repetition pervasive in reading instruction was rivaled by mathematical activities. In an era when personal calculators were still decades in the future, a passerby could have heard children shouting in unison a numerical litany based on "times tables" (four times six is twenty-four, five times six is thirty, etc.), suggesting that with enough repetition a child could become a human calculator with an array of correct answers readily on call.

If the typical fifties elementary school curriculum concentrated on reading and mathematical skills, the school day was peppered with a variety of other activities. The recently ended world war and the ongoing cold war with the Soviet Union, China, and assorted client states encouraged attention to history, geography, and basic government structure (often called "civics"). American history was presented in the traditional heroic model of triumph over British tyranny, struggle for existence on the frontier, and the rise of cities and industrialization, but two major themes differed substantially from the experience of the Boomers' parents. First, of course, was the enormous impact of World War II, which seemed to straddle a position between history and current events. Since students were often encouraged to use parents as resources for war-related projects, and virtually all teachers had experienced the conflict on some personal level, the period could often occupy a significant portion of the history curriculum in the upper grades of elementary school.

The second change, just beginning to emerge in the 1950s, was a consideration of individuals and groups that had been underrepresented in earlier generations of history teaching. The exploits and accomplishments of Native Americans, African Americans, and women were now beginning to be interwoven into the tapestry of the American experience, even if the process was often tentative and occupied a relatively small portion of the narrative.

A category increasingly identified as social studies was heavily influenced by the nation's sudden emergence as a superpower and the reality of its competition with the Communist bloc. Civics courses often presented American democratic government in sharp contrast to the tyranny of communism while geography texts sometimes contrasted the experience of a typical American family with the far harsher existence to be found on a Soviet commune. Geography textbooks with titles such as *Our Latin American Neighbors* emphasized the strategic products of these nations; textbooks on European geography frequently displayed bold lines of demarcation dividing Western Europe from the nations behind the Iron Curtain.

Probably the most disturbing element of the 1950s social studies curriculum was an experience that was never tested or graded. This was the grim preparation for a possible nuclear attack launched from the Soviet Union. One of the most commonly shared experiences of almost all early Boomers was the shrill wail of sirens attached to the ritual known as "duck and cover." World War II–era pupils had been the first American children exposed to the possibility of enemy air bombardment of their schools and homes, but after the initial panic following Pearl Harbor, the threat of a serious Axis bombing of the mainland United States receded to the point that air raid drills became little more than a welcome relief from a scheduled spelling test.

It would be the Baby Boomers, the first cold-war kids, who would see animated and live "educational" films that graphically demonstrated what an atomic bomb could do to a largely defenseless public. Some classrooms featured post-

Most schoolchildren of the cold-war period became experienced veterans of duck-and-cover activities. Even the animated advice of Bert the Turtle and the suggestion that part of the exercise was in preparation for a natural disaster could not conceal the grim possibility of nuclear war. *(Bettmann/CORBIS)*

ers that displayed an aerial map of the nearest major city with concentric rings showing the level of destruction to be expected if a nuclear weapon were dropped in the center of the city. Teachers affecting a matter-of-fact detachment sometimes helped pupils calculate the severity of damage to their school or neighborhood, depending on its distance from ground zero. Children went from week to week without knowing when the eerie whine of sirens would announce reality, signaling the end of the world they knew.

Tensions between the United States and the Soviet Union never deteriorated to the point where the protection of school desks against atomic attack was tested. Yet, just as the oldest Boomer children settled into their sixth-grade routine, a real threat from the skies rocked the American school system to its core. On Friday, October 4, 1957, the Soviet space agency successfully launched the first man-made object to achieve orbit around the Earth. A Soviet R-7 rocket lifted from the ground with a thunderous roar as five engines supplied over a million pounds of thrust. Speeding at more than 17,000 miles an hour, the rocket reached an altitude of 142 miles and released a 184-pound sphere studded with four antennae. Seconds later, radio signals beamed toward Earth with a distinct beeping sound. Soviet premier Nikita Khrushchev soon announced to the world that the age of space exploration had begun with a "demonstration of the advantage of socialism in actual practice."

The launch of Sputnik was a fantastic propaganda triumph for the Soviet Union. Every ninety-six minutes a vehicle bearing a hammer-and-sickle insignia passed over the planet in an orbit that allowed Americans from New York City to Kansas an opportunity to glimpse mankind's first tentative baby steps into the cosmos. American newspapers and commentators gave a grudging compliment to their ideological rivals: "Orbiting with an eerie intermittent croak that sounds like a cricket with a cold, picked up by radio receivers around the world, Sputnik passes through the stratosphere on an epochal journey."

When American children returned to school the following Monday, the repercussions of this achievement were already creeping into the classroom. During much of the preceding decade a significant portion of American educational thought had argued that American children were exposed to a curriculum that sacrificed essential academic skills in favor of socialization, peer acceptance, and marginally beneficial school activities. Now books such as *Why Johnny Can't Read*, lamenting the shortcomings of American schools, were joined by *What Ivan Knows That Johnny Doesn't* and *The Little Red Schoolhouse*, which promised to divulge what

Soviet schools did right. *Life* magazine spent much of the 1957–1958 school year publishing cover stories on "The Crisis in Education," filled with comparison photos of Russian and American school activities. One pair of images showed a group of serious-minded Soviet children huddled over an imposing array of scientific equipment, contrasted with an American classroom where carefree students were learning the newest popular dance. An educational journal noted that "up to Sputnik, Little Ivan, just like little Johnny, went to school period, no story, no comment, and no one gave a hoot about the fact that Ivan was learning not quite the same thing in school as Johnny. Now we have the 'Cold War Classroom' with press lines almost to the point of hysteria, as average Americans cannot believe that the educational effort of 'backward Russia with savage Communist masters' could be so significant and important."

Events over the next few months merely added to the growing sense of alarm. On the eve of the anniversary of the Russian Revolution in early November, Sputnik II was launched, and the thousand-pound sphere carried the first space passenger, a female terrier named Laika, who was placed in a pressurized cabin equipped with food dispensers and water. Laika did not survive a partial power failure, but the sound of a dog barking inside the massive craft scored another impressive Soviet propaganda triumph.

A December 1957 American launch attempt produced a stark contrast in space technology when the Vanguard rocket exploded into thousands of pieces, barely fifty feet above the Cape Canaveral launch pad. On the last day of January 1958 the United States salvaged a measure of pride when an army Jupiter rocket carried an 80-inch-long cylinder named Explorer I into successful orbit. America had entered the space race, and Explorer achieved an orbit an impressive 1,563 miles above Earth. Yet its 30-pound, six-inch-diameter size seemed puny, and the launch did little to convince many Americans that Soviet schools were not outperforming American institutions. While many proposals for educational reform were focused on colleges and high schools, millions of Boomer elementary school children would be affected by Sputnik.

Salt Lake City became one of the first school districts to add Russian to its elementary school curriculum. Children at Bonneville Elementary School were profiled studying the rather exotic language by using Soviet textbooks, since no Russian texts were currently printed in the United States. Because Soviet texts were filled with pro-Communist propaganda, questionable paragraphs were cut out with razor blades. One cheerful pupil insisted, "This will help me get a good job with the government." In Oklahoma City, TV station KBTA gave Russian courses for grade-school children three days a week while Portland, Oregon, elementary school kids peered through a telescope set up in a teacher's garden as every morning at 6 A.M. they watched for Sputnik to pass over.

The Sputnik launch produced a barrage of calls for more toughness and rigor in American elementary schools. Substantial increases in foreign language, physical education, and science, down to the first-grade level, could be accomplished by cutting back on art and music instruction. Homework assignments could be substantially increased. The school year could be lengthened, and calls for that bane of childhood, year-round school, floated from one community to another. Yet most of these urgings proved to be less intrusive than children feared or educators hoped. Much of the new science education in elementary schools tended to be more fun than drudgery. For example, a Riverside, California, elementary school quickly developed a science fair based on space exploration. A photo image shows a crowd of children, faces half hidden under cardboard space helmets, constructing a thirteen-foot-high cardboard rocket, control panel, and launching pad designed for a mock trip to the moon, while their delighted teacher insists that such activities will encourage students to "think mathematically." Many young children were now determined to become astronauts, and new heroes were the handsome rocket scientist Wernher von Braun (a German refugee) and soon the astronauts Alan Shepard and John Glenn. Year-round schools, shorter vacations, and lengthened school days sounded frightening to an average ten-year-old Boomer child; but, in a mix of wishful thinking and almost adult perspective, these same ten-year-olds reasoned that their teachers too would not welcome year-round school and longer school days. Recreational and amusement interests would challenge the loss of revenue, and parents could never take a family vacation if holiday periods were staggered among different grades. In this case the kids were more on target about the real world than many educational theorists. While some school districts tinkered with their schedules, most Boomer children would retain their long summer vacations and mid-afternoon dismissals. On weekday afternoons and evenings, weekends, holiday breaks, and summer vacations, these postwar children would enter a world far removed from school. Their play and recreation would be nostalgically remembered a half-century later.

4

LEISURE WORLD

THE IMAGES of a young generation at play in the 1950s are impossible to avoid: freckle-faced boys adjusting Mickey Mouse ears or Davy Crockett coonskin caps, giggling girls gyrating to the motion of colorful Hula Hoops, smiling children leaning out of the windows of the family station wagon as they near a beach resort or picnic grounds. Whatever the specific type of activity, the Boomers, like most children of any generation, were engaged in an adventure that expanded their horizons outward from their homes to the nation or world at large. Yet, more than most previous generations, this very act of recreation and exploration encouraged massive adult discussion, debate, and commentary. The birth of 76 million children between 1946 and 1964 produced an enormous incentive to channel the energies of this youth tidal wave into positive directions. But for the main players in this drama, the kids, the leisure world of the 1950s would produce a nostalgia that would stay with them through their adult lives.

The boys and girls who would become the parents of the Boomers had already experienced their own magical world of play in the 1930s and 1940s. They had listened to Little Orphan Annie on the radio, read Nancy Drew and the Hardy Boys books, followed comic-book heroes, and watched Dorothy travel from Kansas to Oz. Their world had offered Shirley Temple dolls, Red Ryder toy rifles, and Big Little books. But the magical world always had finite limits as depression and war instilled the need to sacrifice and make do with less. Now the prewar children had sons and daughters of their own, and much of the 1950s would be spent in an emotional tug-of-war. While the booming economy offered parents the opportunity to give their children more than they had experienced, the austerity of their own childhoods suggested that kids who received too much would become spoiled brats, unable to function well in a still conservative society.

The first hint that the Boomer generation would spend at least part of their leisure time differently from their parents could be seen in the transition in living-room furniture. The children of the 1930s and World War II had formed the one and only "radio generation." The first decade of commercial radio broadcasting in the twenties held little of interest for children as the medium focused on news, farm reports, sports events, and recorded music. The more iconic programs—comedies, mysteries, and, above all, children's shows—began in the early to mid-thirties. Boys and girls sprawled on living-room floors and lounged on couches or chairs, always with their attention directed to the radio set that held pride of place in the parlor. The sons and daughters of the "radio kids" generation also sprawled and lounged in much the same positions, but their attention was focused on a flickering black-and-white screen that replaced the radio as the magic carpet to new worlds and adventures.

The first children's television hit show: the interaction between live actress Fran Allison and puppets Kukla and Ollie not only entranced postwar children but brought many adults into a charming and magical world that demonstrated the potential of the new medium. *(Time & Life Pictures/Getty Images)*

Remarkable new characters entranced Boomers and even their parents before the kids could even pronounce their names. Burr Tillstrom, a thirty-two-year-old puppeteer, teamed with Fran Allison, a middle-aged former teacher, radio singer, and actress, to present NBC's huge hit *Kukla, Fran and Ollie*. Allison was the human mediator between Kukla, a balding, beetle-browed puppet with an efficient, slightly superior air, and Ollie, a dragon with one tooth and a playboy personality who was a severe trial to Kukla's patience. "It is the undeniable opinion of many television set owners," one magazine wrote, "that this is the most delightful program on the air." For the first time in history, young parents could sit next to their wide-eyed children in their own living room and, for a moment, learn once again how much fun it was to believe in the other realities their television set offered.

Tillstrom and Allison soon had competition in the form of another, more frenetic human-marionette interchange. *The Howdy Doody Show* featured a live audience of exuberant preschoolers seated in a row of bleachers called the Peanut Gallery. The two stars of the daily show were genial, burly "Buffalo Bob" Smith, dressed in a Western-style fringe outfit, and his puppet counterpart, Howdy Doody, a frecklefaced redheaded boy dressed in miniature plaid shirt, neckerchief, and blue jeans. Buffalo Bob's major nemesis was the irrepressible clown Clarabelle, who communicated only through honks of a horn while spraying victims with seltzer bottles, while Howdy's antagonist in the town of Doodyville was the mean, supercilious banker Phineas T. Bluster. The show was fast-paced yet gentle. By episode's end, Clarabelle would behave, Mr. Bluster would prove capable of good deeds and empathy, and the television audience would learn much about friendship and conflict resolution.

Kinescope recordings of *Kukla, Fran and Ollie* and *Howdy Doody* often appear primitive compared to *Sesame Street* and *The Electric Company*, yet for the first cohorts of Boomers and many of their parents they offered access to an almost unlimited universe beyond the home. Because television was so new, it carried some of the same shared wonder now produced by the internet. Even as these original programs gave way to more sophisticated fare, some portion of the special bond between television and the first generation that grew up with the medium would remain.

Television is the leisure activity most associated with children of the fifties and early sixties, not because it was

the Boomers' dominant recreation—it probably was not—
but because of their unique status as the first "TV generation." The limited number of channels in the precable era,
the limited hours each station broadcast, and the limited
number of television sets in each household ensured that
the youngsters of this era could never match their children
or grandchildren in the opportunity to watch television almost continuously. Yet these very limitations created a much
stronger sense of shared community, an almost village-like
experience of viewing in which family members, friends,
and schoolmates often watched the same program so that
discussion of a particular show might carry over from the
living room to the schoolyard the next day. The viewing of
some evening programs became family events.

Boomer children would generally participate in three
sometimes distinct but overlapping television experiences:
children's television, specifically directed at young viewers,
in which adults were merely tolerated; family programs,
which sought to attract both children and their parents; and
adult-oriented shows geared for a more mature audience
but either surreptitiously or openly viewed by children as a
glimpse of a world beyond childhood. Television viewing was
also a changing universe: the oldest Boomers gradually left
the more juvenile shows to their younger siblings, and the
networks frequently canceled programs and forced children
to experiment with a new show, so that no two television
seasons were ever exactly alike. Yet even if the world of early
television was hardly static, there were enough characteristic programs or formats to provide insight into the Boomers'
viewing experience.

The children's programs on the networks (NBC, CBS,
ABC, and, early on, DuMont) usually featured action geared

to short attention spans, sometimes used children as important characters, and advertised products aimed at a young audience. Children's programs could be live, animated, or a combination of the two, and would usually be broadcast weekday mornings, afternoons, or early evenings, and Saturday morning, either live or on film.

The most successful weekday children's program of the 1950s was the *Mickey Mouse Club*, which captured the attention of much of the young population of that era. The program featured a cast dominated by talented, photogenic children between eight and twelve years of age, who danced and sang in almost vaudevillian routines, introduced by the only significant adult presence, Jimmy Dodd. While all the Mouseketeers quickly enjoyed fan clubs, a few children became early idols of Boomer kids. The two youngest performers, eight-year-olds Cubby O'Brien and Karen Pendleton, were precocious, cute, and the only kids who were actual Boomers themselves. Twelve-year-olds Annette Funicello and Tommy Kirk were the most versatile, which led them to post-Mousketeer acting and singing careers. One of the most attractive elements of the program was that each day had a separate theme, such as "Fun with Music" day, and stage action was interspersed with filmed serials, such as Spin and Marty and the Hardy Boys episodes. Product tie-ins to the series were heavily advertised, and millions of children clamored for the attachable mouse ears that would become one of the symbolic images of Boomer childhood.

The hugely successful *Mickey Mouse Club* usually led into more localized children's fare in the time slots just before or even during dinnertime. Many local stations found a profitable niche for recycled 1930s and 1940s comedy shorts and cartoons, so that many Boomer children watched various *Three Stooges Shows* and *Popeye Theaters* hosted by local personalities. More than a few perplexed children tried to decipher Swing Era slang and jokes or wondered why Popeye was fighting 1950s allies such as the Germans or Japanese. Daily afternoon programs were followed by early evening prime-time shows that emphasized a family-friendly or child-friendly component. *Rin Tin Tin, Lassie, My Friend Flicka,* and *Circus Boy* were filmed dramatic series in which the central characters were children, often orphaned or in a single-parent home, and frequently paired with a highly intelligent animal. The evening time slots of these programs ensured at least some level of adult audience, and commercials were a mix of general family products and items of specific interest to children.

Prime-time children's programs either competed with or led into the broadest category of network television programming, shows developed for the entire family with sponsors geared to adult purchase. Ten years after the first tentative steps toward network broadcasting, a fairly standardized series of formats began to dominate mid-evening family viewing. A glance at a network program grid from 1957 reveals a variety of formats centered on programs that would become icons of fifties popular culture. Situation comedies such as *I Love Lucy, Father Knows Best,* and *Ozzie and Harriet*; Westerns such as *Maverick, Wyatt Earp,* and *Sugarfoot*; and comedy/variety programs including Jackie Gleason, Red Skelton, and George Gobel were eagerly anticipated events for all age groups. Only the enormously popular and mostly rigged quiz-show format of *Twenty-One, Sixty-Four Thousand Dollar Question,* and *Tic Tac Dough* was an endangered species, and as congressional pressure forced their cancellation, they were quickly replaced by *Donna Reed, Leave It to Beaver,*

The situation comedies of the postwar era, like *Leave It to Beaver*, became a shared experience for all members of Boomer-era families, even if real households were considerably larger than their TV counterparts. *(Getty Images)*

and *Bonanza*. Generally Westerns had enough action and comedies offered enough slapstick or young characters that children were entranced, even if the advertisements were for floor wax or deodorant. Since rules governing bedtime varied by household, not all kids saw all of these programs, yet a family audience encouraged a discussion about shows that attracted children as listeners or participants, far more than twenty-first-century parents might imagine.

For most children, the least accessible television programming was the increasingly mature fare after 9 or 10 P.M. Even the most "adult" drama then would receive a PG rating in modern coding, but many fifties parents were nonetheless concerned about the impact of television on their children. Some children who were able to negotiate lenient terms from their parents were sometimes permitted to sample "adult" programs such as *Perry Como* or *Andy Williams*, simply because the "mature" character of the program was its music content, which would be supremely boring to a ten-year-old. Slightly older children might be permitted to stay up late enough to view weekend episodes of moderately scary but not particularly violent or suggestive shows, such as *One Step Beyond* or *Twilight Zone*. Programs that were extremely violent or sexually suggestive, however, represented the parental line in the sand, as the furor over the body count and implied sexuality of the late fifties program *The Untouchables* testified. Still, this reality was far removed from V-chips and parental lockboxes, and children's viewing habits tended to remain rather tightly under adult control and supervision.

By the late 1950s more than 90 percent of households had television sets. Yet many of children's leisure-time activities exhibited direct continuity with those of prewar youngsters. In the summer, for example, many beach resorts, camping areas, and other vacation spots were too far from cities with television stations to provide viewing opportunities. And more than a few parents felt that in summertime their children should be doing something other than watching reruns, so that in many cases the breakdown-prone TV sets weren't repaired, or adults imposed stringent viewing restrictions during vacation months.

One classic prewar activity in a world of limited television channels and summer "blackouts" was that other visual medium, the motion picture. Postwar children had fewer movie theaters and fewer films than their parents had enjoyed in their childhoods, but most of the thirties and forties movie experience was still largely intact. Much like their parents' era, Boomer movie viewing was roughly divided into two experiences, Saturday matinees for kids and evening shows with parental accompaniment.

Urban or suburban neighborhood theaters accessible by foot or bicycle, and newer theaters in shopping centers that catered to auto traffic, both provided that staple of childhood recreation, the Saturday matinee. These shows offered a low admission price, often a quarter or half-dollar, and tended to have an audience composed primarily of children, with older siblings chaperoning younger brothers or sisters. The features often included one or two low-budget comedies, such as *Ma and Pa Kettle* or *Francis the Talking Mule*, or equally low-budget science fiction, horror, or World War II films, supplemented by strings of cartoons that offered the advantage of being in color in the theater while on television they were only black and white. Many parents were happy to unload some or all of their children for a Saturday afternoon, much to the consternation of harried ushers and candy-counter personnel. Altogether the experience was close to what the Boomers' parents had known in the 1930s—and even their grandparents remembered from the silent-film era.

The family outing to a movie theater in the evening, a major part of social life in the 1930s and during World War II, continued to be a major event throughout the fifties and early sixties. The film industry was initially terrified that the advent of television would remove the incentive for families to leave the house and pay for watching films. These fears were partially realized: two or three visits to the Bijou now became a more occasional, yet more special, event. Three film genres were still able to entice mother and dad to take the children to the movies. First was the "spectacular," using new technologies in sound and wide screen, often involving a film with religious or moral overtones. Among the most successful films in this category were *The Ten Commandments* and *Ben Hur*. The second theme focused on Walt Disney's ability to entice families to view a combination of re-released and new animated features. In the postwar era parents relived *Dumbo* and *Snow White* with their children while all experienced first-time screenings of *Lady and the Tramp* and *Sleeping Beauty*. Finally, Disney and some competing companies updated the prewar family comedy and adventure movies, offering the added attraction of a wide screen and color, not available at home. These offerings included *The AbsentMinded Professor* and, remarkably, a compilation of the three-episode television presentation of *Davy Crockett*. A final postwar movie theme, developed with little concern for a young audience yet experienced by a great many Boomer children, centered on adult tastes in music. The fifties and early sixties were replete with biographies of famous big-bandleaders, such as *The Benny Goodman Story* and *The Glenn Miller Story*, and film versions of Broadway musicals such as *My Fair Lady* and *The King and I*. All these films offered catchy tunes and relatively accessible plot lines, but this part of the "family" movie experience was probably more memorable for the parents than the kids.

If television represented the most visible break with earlier childhood leisure activities, and movies maintained the most significant bridge between the generations, the toy and game industry offered traditional play activities as well as new experiences. The parents of the Boomers had grown up in a period when a cornucopia of toys were mass produced and heavily advertised on radio, in newspaper ads, and in increasingly colorful catalogues. The children of the 1930s who lived in families that were less damaged by the depression had access to erector sets, electric trains, Shirley Temple dolls, Red Ryder toy rifles, and Monopoly games. Many of these toys were colorful, sturdy, and durable, if also made of relatively expensive materials that limited their accessibility. If metal toy dirigibles, electric trains, and dollhouses represented the Age of Metal, Boomer children would be the first to encounter the Age of Plastic. It is no coincidence that the most popular range of train accessory buildings for budding railroad tycoons of the fifties and sixties was labeled "Plasticville," and offered distinctive postwar structures such as "Tasty Freeze" ice cream stands, spacious supermarkets, and even pastel-colored motels, producing a far different rail layout than the tin litho structures of the thirties. And while Boomer children continued to develop holiday and birthday lists around Sears, Macy's, Lionel, or American Flyer catalogues, television advertising now allowed them to see their desired toys in action, which hardly discouraged demand.

The large numbers of children coupled with an escalating number of toy lines produced conflicting tastes. Children argued whether Lionel or American Flyer made the best trains, whether Ideal or Mattel made more realistic dolls, and whether Milton Bradley's Easy Money was superior to Parker Brothers' Monopoly. Still, it is possible to paint a broad canvas of the postwar generation at play.

One common element of Boomers at play was the formalization of traditional role-playing, encouraged by the emergence of relatively inexpensive plastic toys. Role-playing included historical re-creations, such as the Wild West and the recently ended World War II; contemporary adult occupations, such as physician or nurse; and a speculative yet exciting future revolving around space exploration that, at least theoretically, might become reality during the children's adult lives.

The prewar interest in frontier exploits, transmitted by numerous films and radio programs, became even more pronounced in the fifties and sixties. Not only were there big-budget color movies, but television rapidly became a giant corral for Western series. By 1959 twenty-six prime-time series were concerned with frontier life, with nearly twenty other syndicated Western programs airing on Saturday morning and weekday early evenings. Many of these shows, including *Bonanza*, *Gene Autry*, and *Roy Rogers*, had extensive toy company tie-ins that allowed boys and girls to reenact the Wild West in their own homes or neighborhoods with cowboy or cowgirl hats, fringed jackets, boots, and authentic-looking weapons.

Most Boomers had at least one parent who had been actively involved in some aspect of World War II, and while some of these men and women were reluctant to discuss their experiences, many others served as models for role-playing activities. A degree of realism was provided when the toy companies' weapons and accessories were supplemented by children's use of their parents' canteens, helmets, rank insignia, and even uniform articles, as imaginary Axis replaced Western outlaws as adversaries.

The postwar period saw role-playing in a future world seriously challenge the reenactment of historical events in children's play experiences. Boomers' parents had had a taste of science fiction with the comic-strip and film serials of Buck Rogers and Flash Gordon and related toy spin-offs. But the "Atomic Age" of the fifties and early sixties prompted a quantum leap in these activities among postwar children. This was the first golden age of science fiction films with robots, spaceships, and futuristic weapons featured in movies such as *Forbidden Planet*, *Invaders from Mars*, and *This Island Earth*, and in television programs such as *Tom Corbett—Space Cadet*, *Space Patrol*, and *The Jetsons*. Along with the real-life exploits of Sputnik and NASA's Mercury programs was the imaginative extrapolation of these events by children.

While one aspect of role-playing was based on children becoming actors in a mini-drama, ranging from contemporary medical care to wartime combat, another major element of this experience was to use toys as surrogates in a miniaturized version of real or imaginary events. In the fifties and early sixties, girls often created this "small world" through dolls, boys through action figures and model railroads.

One of the most notable effects of the postwar revolution in plastics was the greater sophistication of dolls and related accessories available to Boomer girls. Prewar girls might have thought it marvelous that their doll could open and close its eyes, but postwar dolls could require diaper changes (Betsey Wetsy) and even hold a minor conversation (Chatty Cathy). The age of plastics also created a miniature modern household universe in which sinks had working faucets that sprayed real water, refrigerators had tiny ice-cube trays, and stoves had battery-operated burners that lit up like a real oven. Just as their mothers were managing an increasingly complex household, daughters were mirroring much of this experience in miniature, on a level unheard of even a generation earlier.

Probably the most pervasive doll-oriented development of the era occurred just as the oldest Boomer girls were making the transition from childhood to adolescence. At the very

The booming toy industry of the fifties and sixties encouraged young girls to replicate many aspects of their mothers' homemaking experience. *(Lambert, Hulton Archive)*

end of the 1950s the Mattel Corporation introduced the Barbie doll, which instead of looking like a baby or toddler, was designed to be an attractive, fashion-conscious teenager. Along with boyfriend Ken and little sister Skipper, Barbie offered the possibility of a miniature teen life, with so many wardrobe changes and accessories that Mattel would soon emerge as one of the leading American clothing manufacturers. Barbie would take the role-playing of doll activities from simulated motherhood to a primer in adolescent relationships just as Boomer girls were making this transition themselves.

As girls' role-playing was increasingly defined by Barbie, Boomer boys were initiated into a more warlike competition with the emergence of G.I. Joe. Before the postwar boom in plastic toys, boys had created a military universe through lead or tin toy soldiers and a transportation universe of metal cars, trucks, and model railroads. One significant limitation of these generally sturdy, colorful toys was that they were so expensive that a child's "army" might include only twenty or thirty soldiers or cowboys, and home rail empires were limited to one or two trains and a handful of buildings. This situation began to alter radically during the decades after World War II. Toy companies such as Marx began selling new plastic figures ranging from 35 mm to 60 mm in size for a nickel or a dime each, while combining elaborate sets, including figures, forts, buildings, and accessories, for about five dollars. These included play sets based on television programs, such as a Fort Apache set from *Rin Tin Tin* and Nottingham Castle from *Robin Hood*, as well as World War II and contemporary military forces. In the wake of Barbie's success, toy companies enlarged the size of the figures to six to twenty-four inches and offered changes of uniforms, weapons, accessories, and other features in a figure that was rapidly emerging as a military doll. The most iconic of these figures, G.I. Joe, set the stage for an action-figure boom that would explode during the 1970s with the emergence of the *Star Wars* films.

The arrival of 76 million children between 1941 and 1964 guaranteed that Barbie and G.I. Joe would not be the only new toys to tempt boys and girls. Toy companies delighted children, and sometimes their parents, with Mr. Potato Head, Slinky, Hula Hoops, Twisters, Wiffle ball sets, and Silly Putty. Some game manufacturers introduced Scrabble, Battleship, The Game of Life, and an "electronic" football game where miniature red and yellow players seemed to circle endlessly on a green metal gridiron. Game shows, such as *Concentration*, *Tic Tac Dough*, and *Dotto*, promoted their home versions. The profusion of new toys meant that children's wish lists often grew so long that even relatively affluent parents had to disappoint their children.

The emergence of television and the expansion of the toy inventory convinced many teachers and parents that the era of reading for pleasure was largely over. In one sense they were correct, as curling up with a book was no longer the only diversion on a rainy afternoon or a snowy evening. Yet television channels and broadcast times were still relatively limited, and toy boxes were not quite so overflowing that children could not still be tempted to escape to a world of print that was at once familiar and new to their parents.

Books that bridged the time between the 1930s and the 1950s included *The Bobsey Twins*, *Nancy Drew*, and *The Hardy Boys* series, which often included new cover artwork but otherwise remained as popular to Boomer children as to their parents. On the other hand, comic strips and comic books were undergoing more significant changes. By the end of the fifties a few prewar comic strips still inhabited the Sunday comics section of the newspaper, as *Blondie*, *Mutt and Jeff*, and *Henry* still attracted kids' attention. But newer strips, including *Beetle Bailey*, *Dennis the Menace*, and *Peanuts* were emerging as stars. Most newspapers could carry only a finite number of daily and Sunday comics, and *Katzenjammer Kids*, *Little Orphan Annie*, *Buck Rogers*, and other icons of the thirties often surrendered their places to a new generation of characters.

The world of comic books was somewhat less constrained as the number of publications was limited only to the ability of children to afford them. Therefore many of the most visible comic heroes of the thirties remained more or less intact a generation later. *Superman, Batman, Wonder Woman,* and *The Flash* were still very popular, but plot lines changed in several areas. Superman's enemies tended to be extraterrestrials rather than gangsters, as befitting the emergence of atomic power and possible space exploration. The Man of Steel had also acquired a female teenage cousin who was soon featured in her own comic book. Supergirl joined Lois Lane as a strong female role model with her own plot lines where Superman was a relatively peripheral character. Also, in an ironic twist, D.C. Publishers launched a *Superboy* comic book chronicling adventures in the Smallville of the 1930s, which had been the contemporary time frame of the original adult character.

As fifties and sixties superheroes were called upon to deal increasingly with visitors from outer space, as opposed to gangsters or spies, publishers added anthology-oriented science fiction comic books, such as *Strange Adventures* and *Mystery in Space.* The relatively few continuing characters in these publications possessed no supernatural powers but were usually ordinary individuals faced with extraordinary situations, such as the Atomic Knights, who used specially treated suits of armor to survive the distant post-nuclear-war future of 1999.

While this was considered the "Silver Age" of comic book superheroes, many Boomer children paid just as much attention to more comedy-oriented comic books. *Archie, Nancy, Little Lulu,* and *Dennis the Menace* were all top-selling franchises. Walt Disney used comic books to feature characters that were less prominent in his on-screen cartoons, probably the best-selling feature being Donald Duck's mischievous nephews Huey, Dewey, and Louie, and Donald's rich, cantankerous uncle, Scrooge McDuck. This quartet largely pushed Donald to the background in the comic book universe and introduced characters that would become particularly identified with the Boomer generation.

The combination of television, a much wider range of affordable toys, a significant increase in child-oriented films, and the expansion of children's book and comic-book titles guaranteed that Boomer children would have access to a cornucopia of leisure activities unprecedented in the nation's history. Yet the sheer size of this generation of children persuaded more than a few parents that organized, adult-directed activities were the best antidote to watching a youth culture spin out of control.

The fifties and sixties were a time not only of Hula Hoops and hopscotch but also of Little League, Brownies, Cub Scouts, and Campfire girls, when the true prototype of "soccer moms" and "football dads" emerged on the American scene. The casual pickup game on the local sandlot gradually gave way to the Tri-State Laundry Cubs meeting the Pepsi-Cola Yankees in a contest directed by adult coaches and supervised by adult umpires. Little Leagues in turn soon shared attention with Pop Warner football, Biddy Basketball, and a number of youth soccer leagues. A smaller but growing parallel universe of softball, basketball, soccer, and cheerleading programs attracted thousands of young girls to organized sports.

Millions of Boomers seamlessly traded baseball or cheerleading uniforms for the blue shirts and yellow neckerchiefs of Cub Scouts or the brown beanies of Brownies, as scouting seemed to grow in geometric progression with young moms shuttling between den-mother duties for their sons and helping distribute Girl Scout cookies with their daughters.

As in any cross-generational conversation, it is not difficult to imagine the children and grandchildren of the Boomer generation rolling their eyes in disbelief as middle-aged adults fondly recount watching grainy black-and-while television programs or playing with decidedly low-tech toys. Children of more recent decades, exposed to a sensory bombardment of video games, high-definition cable television, and iPods, wonder how anyone could have had fun in a far more unplugged era. Yet the iconic images of midcentury childhood—Hula Hoop contests, smiling children in Davy Crockett caps, and mesmerized attention to the antics of Howdy Doody—are not illusions or gross exaggerations. The children of that era somehow instinctively knew that they lived in a magical time that could never be fully replicated. Boomer children certainly captured the attention of the adult world in the fifties. The one complicating factor was that these kids were fated to share the spotlight with slightly older youngsters who in some cases were their brothers and sisters. These siblings were producing their own iconic images as America's first "teenagers."

5

SIBLING RIVALRY

ONE OF THE IRONIES of the Boomer childhood experience in the 1950s was that postwar children had to share center stage in the youth culture arena with older siblings and neighbors who spent the same decade emerging as the nation's first real "teenage" generation. Pictures of Boomer kids in Mickey Mouse ears and twirling inside Hula Hoops always seemed to compete with images of Elvis Presley, James Dean, and teen girls in poodle skirts. If postwar kids had the edge in sheer numbers, the emerging teenage generation had age and spending money on its side in this friendly generational rivalry. On one side were real-life versions of Jeff Stone, "Beaver" Cleaver, and "Kitten" Anderson, kids making their way through the fifties as children and preteens. Their older siblings were the new generation of teens portrayed on television by Mary Stone, Wally Cleaver, and "Princess" Anderson in a variety of same-sex and opposite-gender squabbles that stopped just long enough to form a united front against parents or other adult authority figures.

Fifties Boomers and teenagers shared common neighborhoods, common homes, and even common bedrooms, but they experienced the first full postwar decade at different points in their young lives. The pre-Boomer generation spent much of the fifties collecting Elvis Presley records, showing off leather jackets, cashmere sweaters, pompadours, and ponytails. Contrary to depictions in *Blackboard Jungle* and *Rebel Without a Cause*, most of these young people were well-behaved and polite. Yet they *were* the "first teenagers," and even well-behaved kids scared adults when they swung or shook to the startling rhythms of Chuck Berry or Little Richard.

In the period before World War II, adults generally referred to young people between thirteen and nineteen as "adolescents" or "youth," and possibly drew some comfort from the fact that most of this group would spend at least half of these years working or seeking a job.

During the war, adults cringed at the dress and morals of "Zoot Suiters" and "Victory Girls," but most young people spent the war maturing rapidly as paratroopers or welders or even baby-sitters as they aided the war effort in many ways. By 1944 psychology, sociology, and education textbooks were just beginning to call this age group "teen-agers" (the hyphen was soon dropped), and late that summer *Seventeen* magazine sold out its first issues as it trumpeted the intelligence, energy, and style of this newly defined cohort. Then, as America reached midcentury, a new watershed was reached. For the first time more young people graduated from high school than dropped out, and educators predicted that this percentage would surge during the coming decade. For a brief time in the early fifties it seemed that the only unique aspect of this newly designated group called "teenagers" was their common experience in completing high school more frequently than their parents.

In mid-decade the motion picture industry, the recording industry, radio, and television all began to create or reflect an image of a new cultural subgroup in America, an "invasion of teenagers." The first hints of change occurred with a surge of articles dealing with the rapid increase in juvenile delinquency and juvenile crimes. The phenomenon did not reach the epidemic proportions implied in print, but Hollywood quickly latched onto the theme. A disturbing film of 1953, *The Wild One*, had featured Marlon Brando as an angry, violent member of a motorcycle gang terrorizing a small California town. While Brando and his minions were clearly well past adolescence, the film resonated with some teenagers, and black leather jackets and tight jeans began to enter the periphery of young male fashion. Two years later, in 1955, producers shifted this surly, anti-social behavior to the high school environment and dropped the young rebels' ages from the twenties to their teens. *Rebel Without a Cause* and *Blackboard Jungle* were huge hits, and the opening song in the latter film, "Rock Around the Clock," became the first clearly designated rock-and-roll tune to reach number one in sales in *Billboard* magazine's "Hot 100" survey. At almost the exact moment when Davy Crockett and Mickey Mouse Club mania was producing iconic images of Boomers at play, the media were just as eagerly reporting the new "teenage craze" of rock-and-roll music. Radio stations discovered they could reclaim ratings lost to adult television watchers by adopting a "Top 40" format of new rock-and-roll songs geared to a teenage audience. The genial Bill Haley and his Comets became the first contenders for rock-star status when "Rock Around the Clock," "See You Later Alligator," and "Shake, Rattle and Roll" all emerged as Top 10 songs. The Pennsylvania group was mobbed in London, sold out in West Germany, and was vilified as crazed, capitalist hoodlums on the other side of the Iron Curtain. Yet if Haley's music was enormously popular, he was a little too old and a little too bland to have the sex appeal needed for a truly magnetic superstar. That role would fall to a young Southerner who began a rise to stardom just as the Comets were beginning to fade. Elvis Presley was younger than Bill Haley but just a bit older than mid-fifties teens when he made the transition from regional favorite to national idol. After individual appearances on the *Jimmy Dorsey Hour* (full shot) and the Ed Sullivan Show (waist up), Presley became the focal point of teen music and a demon to some elements of adult society. The singer's slightly snarling demeanor, tight pants, leather jacket, and long sideburns produced a legion of teenage followers and alternately attracted and repelled everyone else. "Heartbreak Hotel," "Hound Dog," and "All Shook Up" were almost impossible to ignore as background music for the mid-decade soundtrack, and for every adult who decried Presley's "sexually suggestive" gyrations, another would emphasize his non-smoking, nondrinking, churchgoing demeanor.

A number of contemporary and more recent narratives of the 1950s have emphasized the generational conflict between teenagers and their new music and a relatively conservative adult society that allegedly looked upon this subculture as a major threat. The real situation was considerably more complex, as both rock-and-roll music and the teens who listened to it formed a complicated entity. Much of adult derision of the new music focused on a relatively few high-profile acts such as the very loud and strange-looking Little Richard (the African American Richard Wayne Pennimay), and the equally loud, equally strange-looking Jerry Lee Lewis, who followed early divorces with a marriage to his early-teen cousin. These twin (yet racially diverse) threats to adult propriety were often coupled with lower-profile, subversion-of-authority songs such as "Get a Job," "Yakety Yak," and "Summertime Blues," which provided detractors with ammunition to emphasize the danger of the new music.

But several contradictory forces seemed to keep the adult protest from reaching a critical mass. First, some of the most popular acts, such as crooner Pat Boone, had an appearance and demeanor that would make them welcome in most adult homes; second, Elvis Presley's army induction and exemplary service dispelled much of the "rebel" myth; and third, the young but incredibly clean-cut Dick Clark quickly emerged as an arbitrator between teen and adult society. Rather symbolically, Clark's Philadelphia-based *American Bandstand* television show was paired in the ABC schedule with the *Mickey Mouse Club* as each program became a fixture for one of the age groups that constituted 1950s childhood.

Clark was neither quite peer nor parent to the teen dancers on *Bandstand*. Rather, he was a responsible older sibling who imposed a strict dress code, inspected report cards, and banned anyone who dropped out of school. The few fifties kinescopes of *Bandstand* still available reveal that the more "rocking" songs and guests were interspersed with a surprisingly large number of ballads by Nat "King" Cole, Perry Como, and other performers who attracted young mothers as well as many teens. The combination of parental viewership and anticipation of the forthcoming Mousketeers activities also meant that a large number of Boomers were at least passively involved in the *Bandstand* experience, even if they were difficult to measure in demographic studies.

The reality of teen music in the fifties, one part Little Richard and Jerry Lee Lewis, another part Pat Boone and Dick Clark, is perhaps a microcosm of the relationship between adults and adolescents in the period. Religious groups and parental organizations decried the sexual content, violence, and anarchism of many teen films, yet virtually every situation comedy had a Mary Stone or Wally Cleaver, whom most adults would have been glad to have in their own home. Newsreels from the era show ministers condemning rock and roll from the pulpit as "jungle music" and adults enthusiastically (with teens less enthusiastically) burning piles of 45 rpm records as if to erase all memory of the awful genre. Yet newspapers and magazines are filled with articles only gently poking fun at teens' activities or lauding their diligence. Most parents and teens in the fifties were clearly aware that some form of social revolution was occurring in the relationship between adults and adolescents, but both sides seemed ripe for compromise, and adults may have suspected that the big change might be exciting and fun.

One episode of the definitive family situation comedy *Ozzie and Harriet* featured the newly emerging rock-and-roll superstar Ricky Nelson discussing the merits of his music with his parents. When Ricky asks his mother's opinion of the new music, Harriet Nelson kiddingly says she can now stay in the same room with Ricky's record player. Then, more seriously, she admits there is plenty of excitement that seems to reflect the emotion of the new teen generation. Similarly, most of the "teenpics" films had far less threatening plots than their advertisements promised. *Blackboard Jungle* ends with a teen—played by Sidney Poitier—and other kids allying themselves with the teacher—played by

Glenn Ford—against the mindless violence of a punk nemesis played by Vic Morrow. *I Was a Teenage Werewolf* and *I Was a Teenage Frankenstein* show the real villains as adult scientists who short-circuit the laws of nature and God while the transformed teens are merely dupes who return to good behavior just before their destruction. *Teenager from Outer Space* produces a revolt of alien adolescents against their adult supervisors, but those adults are planning to conquer Earth, and the teens foil the plot.

Supposedly "subversive" and "satanic" rock-and-roll music appears far less contentious if more than a handful of songs is considered. A perusal of *Billboard*'s Top 10 charts for the first three years of the rock-and-roll experience produces more than a few surprises. Top 40 rock-and-roll radio stations played many hits by such decidedly nonrock artists as Mitch Miller, Nelson Riddle and his Orchestra, Perry Como, Teresa Brewer, Pattie Page, and Doris Day. At the end of 1956, Elvis Presley's "Love Me Tender" was dueling for number one with "True Love" by Bing Crosby and Grace Kelly—hardly symbols of teen rebellion. Even top hits by performers calling themselves "rock-and-roll singers"—"That'll Be the Day" by Buddy Holly, "Bye Bye Love" by the Everly Brothers, and "Little Darlin'" by the Diamonds—provided few opportunities for adult dread of a social revolution. The widely derided teen jargon of the fifties—a litany of "cool," "chicks," and "squares"—seems no more threatening than the "hep" words of the forties or the "23 skidoo" of the twenties, and were more often used in film, television, and records than in everyday teen conversation.

While much has been written about the relationship of fifties teens with the adult world, there has been less interest in the interaction between adolescents and younger children in the era. If the "first teenagers" were perplexing, bewildering, and exasperating to parents, they also evoked a response from their sibling rivals.

One of the first defining realities in the relationship between fifties teenagers and Baby Boomers was whether it was based on family or neighborhood, and this often depended on parents' age and World War II experiences. Boomers with teen siblings tended to have parents who were a bit older than average or fathers who had spent a major portion of their military experience in a stateside assignment. This group included couples who had married in the 1930s and produced children relatively quickly; men who were excused from the draft because they were parents or were employed in critical occupations; or servicemen who were stationed in the United States long enough to be married and have children before the end of the war. Boomers who were acquainted with teenagers only outside the immediate family tended to have parents who had met during the war and delayed marriage or childbirth due to overseas assignments, or had met just after the war and produced postwar children.

By the 1950s most Boomers viewed teenagers with a certain awe and probably saw many of them as "cool," with their greater independence in clothes selection, entertainment, activities, and freedom of movement. On the other hand, in those families where the oldest children were postwar babies and teens were next door or down the street, the adolescents held more of a mystique than in those households where siblings were fighting for bathroom space or privacy in shared bedrooms. In turn, most teens were both more caring and more mature than the characters in period teen films and TV shows, and more than a few felt special protective bonds for siblings or neighbors who had adolescence ahead of them.

Several opportunities helped create a relatively normal bond between the "first teenagers" and the Baby Boomers. First, in the fifties the American public education system was undergoing a massive administrative restructuring in which thousands of school districts transformed the old elementary and high school configuration (K–8, 9–12) into an elementary, junior high, and high school system (K–6, 7–9, 10–12). Boomer children, whose parents may have spent the seventh and eighth grades in single-teacher classrooms in a school with children as young as five, now switched classes, encountered multiple teachers, and interacted with full-fledged teens attending ninth grade. More than a few smaller districts combined junior and senior high schools in the same building, and in some elective subjects, such as creative writing, public speaking, and art, it was possible to have a twelve-year-old sitting next to an eighteen-year-old. Generally these junior high kids were called "preteens," teenagers in training as it were. Their world was very different from the elementary school they had left behind.

A second bonding opportunity emerged as overstretched parents used their teen children to act as parents with some of their younger siblings. Since most teenagers could drive at sixteen, teens could take younger children to doctors' offices, stores, or movies. More than a few boys discovered, to their dismay, that a parental offer of the use of the family car for a date at the drive-in theater might also include a back seat filled with younger siblings, complicating the romantic possibilities for the evening. The numbers of young children provided an expanded opportunity for teens to sample the responsibilities of parenthood, a valuable experience in a society where the average bride was just over nineteen at marriage and the groom not much older.

Finally, Boomers and teens bonded in their mutual fascination with an emerging popular culture that often separated them from the larger adult world. Science fiction and monster movies, television programs aimed at less than mature viewers, and new comic superheroes and satirical publications such as *Mad* magazine provided enormous common ground for prewar, war, and early postwar babies. The more their parents and other adults disparaged those pastimes, the more enjoyable they were for teens and Boomers. Near the end of the fifties, this shared culture gradually began shifting to the tastes of the younger generation. One of the first places it became apparent was in the world of popular music.

By the end of 1958, rock-and-roll music had become a significant element in teenage culture. It featured celebrity performers, inexpensive record players, emerging transistor radio technology, and exposure on national television. Yet within a few months the first incarnation of this new music format was fraying markedly. When impresario Alan Freed's Big Beat Show rock-and-roll concert series played in Boston on May 3, 1958, a frenetic white female member of the audience jumped onto the stage and began embracing a startled black performer in a cross between dancing and sexual contact. An outraged white policeman shoved through the audience toward the stage as security guards began clearing the auditorium. Soon teens and police were skirmishing outside, and media outlets reported a "teen riot."

At about the same time the highly publicized government investigation of corruption in the television quiz-show industry began lapping over into the popular music business. More than a few legislators believed that if game shows were rigged, so was rock and roll. Some disk jockeys, it turned out, lined their pockets while "seducing" teens into listening to particular songs that record companies had bribed them to play. Freed and a number of other pioneer rock-and-roll "DJs" would be professionally ruined by the investigations.

Finally, just after the group Danny and the Juniors followed their smash hit "At the Hop" with the almost euphoric prediction song "Rock and Roll Will Never Die," many of the genre's stars either figuratively or literally did exactly that. In an appalling litany of death notices, Buddy Holly, Richie Valens, the Big Bopper, Eddie Cochran, and Frankie Lymon died, the first three in the same plane crash, Cochran in a British auto accident, and the teenage Lymon in a supposed drug overdose. Chuck Berry found himself fighting gun-possession charges instead of playing his guitar, Little Richard spurned music for the ministry, Jerry Lee Lewis's marriage to his underage cousin was nearly fatal to his career, and the emerging King of rock and roll, Elvis Presley, traded his sideburns for a G.I. crewcut, beginning a two-year stint in the army.

The summer of 1958 not only brought warm breezes across America but the hint that the music the first teenagers called their own was changing, and the new target audience was rapidly becoming the Boomers. At school, picnics, church carnivals, boardwalk hotdog stands, and other recreational activities, loudspeakers and radios blared two new hits that had a rock-and-roll beat but were quickly adopted by children and preteens. David Seville's "Witch Doctor" and Sheb Wooley's "Purple People Eater" were impossible to miss that summer, and both songs essentially parodied serious rock-and-roll love songs with their nonsense premises of a witch doctor as a relationship counselor and a visiting, one-horned alien joining a rock-and-roll band. By mid-June, "Purple People Eater" was the number-one-selling record with "Witch Doctor" close behind. Soon "novelty tunes" dominated radio play lists, as TV horror show host John Zacherle's "Dinner with Drac," the Playmates' satire of car racing, "Beep Beep," Bobby Day's parody of avian teen romance in "Rockin' Robin," and Jan and Dean's lighthearted romance between toddlers in "Baby Talk" were nudging many more serious songs off the radio waves. That 1958 holiday season produced the biggest-selling hit of the year when Seville expanded his "Witch Doctor" nonsense verses into a Christmas wish list from three chipmunks, Theodore, Simon, and the new star of novelty, Alvin. *Alvin and the Chipmunks* albums, toys, and paraphernalia rivaled the earlier Davy Crockett craze and left more than a few teenagers wondering what had happened to their music.

Dick Clark, who had avoided Alan Freed's fall from grace in congressional hearings through a combination of businesslike responses and a well-timed divestment of entangling deals, quickly emerged at the forefront of a changing popular music industry that now viewed Boomer preteens and children as the market of the future while actively toning down those musical elements that seemed to produce adult hostility. By the close of 1959 the young people who had become teenagers during the fifties were turning to a new product, compilation albums of "Golden Oldies," presenting nostalgic collections of songs two or three years old by performers who were no longer the stars of the industry. These teens also became even more deeply connected to the Elvis Presley persona as the King returned from the service in 1960 with films and songs that found a huge audience among his initial fans.

While teenagers who had been old enough to appreciate the excitement of rock and roll in its formative years now often returned to their roots in "Oldies but Goodies," Dick Clark and other promoters were quickly shifting their energies to discover profitable attractions for preteen Boomers. Clark ventured from his *Bandstand* offices to nearby South Philadelphia to discover a quartet of Italian-American teens who had the looks and just enough musical talent to appeal to preadolescent Boomer girls. Fabian Forte, James Darren, Frankie Avalon, and Bobby Rydell all emerged as multimedia phenomena, cutting records, making television appearances, playing supporting roles in general-audience films, and even shooting TV pilots. New York talent scouts countered with Dion DiMucci, Neil Sedaka, and Bobby Darin while fifteen-year-old Paul Anka emerged from his native Montreal as a Canadian-American teen idol. In turn, preteen boys were quickly attracted to Mousketeer Annette Funicello, Connie Francis, and Brenda Lee. Even young television stars who were not primarily singers were encouraged to tap into the new young audience as Connie Stevens of *Hawaiian Eye*, Johnny Crawford of *Rifleman*, and both Shelley Fabares and Paul Peterson of *Donna Reed* enjoyed substantial success in the recording field. Perhaps the most successful of all teen idols was Ricky Nelson, the ebullient younger son of *Ozzie and Harriet*. Under the careful tutelage of his father, Ricky was given substantial time to demonstrate both acting and singing skills on the weekly program, which brought him almost twenty major records and choice movie roles.

The transfer of media interest from fifties teens to Boomer preteens was equally noticeable in the film industry. The peak period of the "teenpics" was 1955 to 1958, yet even in the latter year change was in the air: the great concern with juvenile delinquency was waning. One of the most successful fifties teen movies was *High School Confidential*, which is replete with stock teen characters and jargon. In one scene, a teen hood played by John Drew Barrymore teaches a mock history lesson using only teen language. As the film unfolds, it becomes apparent that the only teen who can outdo Barrymore in confrontational delinquency is a character played by Russ Tamblyn, who is eventually exposed as an undercover police officer. The last major teen film of the fifties, *Because They're Young*, released at the turn of the decade, shifted focus even more dramatically in centering on a young history teacher played by Dick Clark, more than his students, and depicting a high school where the only student wearing a black leather jacket changes to a shirt and tie by the climax of the story. *High School Hellcats* and *Hot Rod Girls* were now largely replaced by much lighter fare directed at preteen Boomer audiences. *The Parent Trap* and *The Misadventures of Merlin Jones* featured Boomer actors such as Hayley Mills and Tommy Kirk.

The change in emphasis is also noticeable in the world of print. Alarming articles of the mid-fifties lamenting juvenile delinquency and teen rebellion faded significantly by the end of the decade. Mainstream magazines now ran features on the pros and cons of preteen dating, the pitfalls of preteen girls attempting to grow up too soon with adult encouragement, and the potential overcrowding of American high schools as the first Boomers reached adolescence. At the same time features on "exotic" or "nonconformist" cultures in America shifted from teens to older subjects such as the Beat Generation. The late fifties and early sixties offered dozens of satirical articles on the newly designated Beatniks, but it was clear that few of them were teenagers.

The fifties teenagers may have been pushed out of the limelight by younger Boomers and older Beatniks, but as they moved toward college and careers they soon realized they had been born at an extremely propitious time. Many more of them were encouraged to attend college in the lull between the G.I. Bill veterans and the looming Boomer generation. When they applied for jobs, they found themselves a small cohort entering a blooming job market. In a slightly ironic twist, the huge teacher shortage created by the Boomers allowed pre-Boomer teacher candidates to have their pick of instructional assignments. A large proportion of Boomer high school and college students would find themselves in classes taught by their still relatively young siblings and neighbors who had been the adolescents of the fifties. And the males of this generation would be too young to serve in the Korean conflict, too old to fight in Vietnam.

The two groups who experienced the 1950s as young people were both adept at befuddling parents and other adults. Each group also represented enormous market potential and became the targets of advertising campaigns, film directors, and television producers. The Boomers often viewed their teenage siblings and neighbors as "cool" and sophisticated, and carefully observed them as they dealt with that formidable entity called the "adult world." In turn, most teenagers saw their younger counterparts as junior admirers and tacit allies in conflicts with parents and authorities. The annoyance of shared bedrooms or crowded recreational facilities was often more than compensated for by parental involvement with the more numerous Boomers, deflecting unwanted attention from the teens.

While these rival siblings had much in common, they would emerge from the fifties with very different perspectives. The teens of the era could still remember a world without television, transistor radios, or jet planes. The older teens could even remember the absent parents, ration coupons, and scrap drives of World War II, and some could even understand the difference between a gold star and a blue star in a neighbor's window. For these young people the magic of the fifties was the magic of transition from child to adolescent, or even from adolescent to young adult. It was the magic of huge pastel-colored cars with tailfins, a new form of music, and new fashions. Those transitions still lay in the future for members of the Baby Boom generation. The Fabulous Fifties were about to give way to what was predicted to be the Soaring Sixties, an era that promised more leisure time, huge communication breakthroughs, and jet airlines crossing the Atlantic. Soon the novelty of writing "1960" in notebooks and class assignments and admiring a new fifty-star flag would set the stage for the ascension of a handsome, incredibly youthful president who had Boomer children of his own exploring their new White House home. The world of Camelot was about to begin, and with its arrival the first postwar babies entered adolescence and their own new world.

6

CAMELOT KIDS

FRIDAY MORNING, January 20, 1961, dawned cold and blustery in Washington, D.C., as the nation's capital joined most of the Northeast in digging out from the third major snowstorm in as many weeks. Yet by noon the White House and the Capitol were bathed in radiant sunshine that produced an almost blinding intensity as it reflected off the new frozen mantle. Residential areas in the city and suburbs teemed with children taking advantage of a snow day to engage in sledding and snowball fights that were relatively unusual in the region. Not far from these frolicking youngsters, a dramatic national event was unfolding. Dwight Eisenhower, at that time the oldest man to serve as president, was about to turn over the reins of government to John F. Kennedy, the youngest man elected to that office.

The newly inaugurated president was a parent of Boomer children and the first occupant of the White House who had been born in the twentieth century. His exceptionally youthful good looks were enhanced by his even younger wife, Jacqueline. The new first couple could have fit comfortably into any gathering of young husbands and wives engaged in managing their exuberant young children while socializing with other adults. As the president delivered his rousing, often-to-be-quoted inaugural speech that was noticeably pitched toward young Americans, the oldest Boomers were midway through their first year of high school while the youngest members of their generation would not be born for nearly another four years. Yet when Kennedy issued his clarion call for young citizens to consider what they could do for their country, not what their country could do for them, the message resonated through an entire generation, however many years they were from voting age.

John and Jacqueline Kennedy's thousand days in the White House would soon be compared to *Camelot*, the smash Broadway musical that chronicled the mythological world of King Arthur and his wife, Guinevere, and their attempts to secure decency and freedom in a barbaric and warlike world. Much like King Arthur's reign, the Kennedy years would emerge as a potent mixture of factual events, speculative theories, and near myth, in which the line between reality and fantasy seemed permanently blurred. For Boomer children this was an appropriate combination, for the first years of the 1960s would offer nostalgic memories and a seductive spectrum of possible alternate realities if destiny had not intruded on a Dallas motorcade.

Boomer families and the Kennedy family were entwined almost immediately. Images of John Jr. crawling under the Oval Office desk, Caroline hunting for Easter eggs on the White House lawn, the grim family vigil as newborn Patrick wavered between life and death—all resonated with young families in the early sixties. For Boomer children, the Kennedy mystique was furthered by photos of touch football on the Hyannis Port beach, presidential promotion of physical

Much of the aura of the Camelot White House was a product of the relation-ship of John and Jacqueline Kennedy and their Boomer children, Caroline and John Jr. *(John F. Kennedy Library)*

fitness in schools, and Kennedy lookalike comedian Vaughn Meader's uncanny duplication of the president's vocal exhortations. Jacqueline Kennedy engaged millions of young mothers as she announced proudly that her children were "Spock babies," and her traditional pillbox hats and bouffant hairstyles set fashion modes in even the smallest communities. Growing up in the Kennedy era would emerge as a major subset of the motion picture industry as Boomers replayed the sounds and the sights of that period in *American Graffiti, Animal House, Dirty Dancing,* and *Hairspray.*

While historians continue to debate whether the Kennedy era was the tail end of the fifties or the precursor of the more radical late sixties, many Boomers old enough to remember those years would agree with neither premise; they would contend that Camelot was simply unique. It was the scariest part of the cold war, with the Berlin Wall and the Cuban Missile Crisis, but it was also a time for new fashions, new music, and new ideas that extended beyond the political and economic aspects of the New Frontier. Somewhere between nostalgia and reality, the Kennedy era seems to provide a tangible bridge between the fifties and the sixties, especially in relation to the youthful concepts of the children who lived through the experience.

During the Kennedy years, postwar babies poured into the secondary school system and by 1963 occupied every grade level from kindergarten to senior high school. For the first time school officials could no longer transfer resources and personnel from less-crowded grades to overcrowded grades; now all grades were overcrowded. Even as new schools were built, finding teachers for them proved difficult as the average stipend of $4,000 a year was still less than enticing for a college graduate who could earn 50 percent more in the private sector. Harried principals played endless academic shell games in their attempts to cover all classes. When a new eleventh-grade English teacher was hired, the principal might shift the incumbent instructor to the still vacant eleventh-grade social studies slot because he or she had taken two or three history courses in college, and that experience might be just enough to keep ahead of the students. Young graduates with biology certification might find themselves teaching even more short-staffed chemistry courses, with vague promises that a certified teacher in that field might eventually be found.

The new president placed education among the top three or four concerns for his administration, and by 1963 school spending had risen to 6 percent of the Gross National Product, compared to 3 percent in 1946. The knowledge industry now rivaled manufacturing as an American activity, as the 50 million students enrolled in schools nearly equaled the number of full-time workers. Beyond the formal classroom, the emergence of communications satellites, cable television, automatic copying machines, and touch-tone telephones signaled the beginning of a new communications revolution that would increasingly affect Boomer children.

Just as these children were offered tantalizing glimpses of a "Jetsons"-like future, they also encountered a glimpse of a possible Armageddon far more terrifying than even the worst days of the Sputnik crisis. Kennedy's predecessor, Dwight Eisenhower, had countered the emotional shock of Soviet space spectaculars and the blustering threats of Soviet chairman Nikita Khrushchev with the calm demeanor of a former military commander who knew that his own country was far stronger. Khrushchev viewed the less experienced, younger Kennedy as more susceptible to threats and nearly ignited a nuclear holocaust. Few Boomers were old enough to understand the intricacies of East-West rivalry over access to West Berlin, the construction of the Berlin Wall, or the discovery of Soviet missiles based in Cuba. What they did see was massive construction of fallout shelters in new schools, national magazine and television features on how to turn family basements into shelters, and grim official hints that "duck and cover" in the classroom might be useless in a Soviet missile barrage that was calculated to kill more than half of all Americans instantly while leaving millions more to die slowly of radiation poisoning.

The classroom Civil Defense films of the fifties had focused on the terrifying but still somehow limited threat of a handful of Soviet bombers penetrating a powerful air defense to drop relatively primitive atomic bombs. Now, as sabers rattled over Berlin or Cuba, even relatively young children were informed that there was simply no defense against an enemy missile that could reach the United States minutes after launch with a payload of death that surpassed that of a hundred 1950s bombers. A frightening film watched by more than a few children in its 1953 release was *Invasion USA*, which depicted a Soviet ground invasion and partial occupation of an unprepared America. A decade later, films such as *On the Beach*, *Dr. Strangelove*, and *Fail-Safe* implied that much or all of the nation might be annihilated in a nuclear conflict.

If there was a moment when Boomers who grew up during the cold war seriously questioned whether they would live to see adulthood, it was during the spectacular autumn of October 1962. Children and teenagers familiar with stark nuclear-test films and multiple episodes of television programs such as *One Step Beyond* and *Twilight Zone*, depicting the many terrors of nuclear war, now saw their nation reach the precipice. On Monday, October 22, with military mobilization and defense alerts as the backdrop, President Kennedy interrupted regular television programming to announce a naval blockade of Cuba and a strong hint that Soviet failure to remove their missiles from that nation might lead to a nuclear exchange. Younger children considering Halloween costume options and teenagers moving toward a driver's license, first date, first kiss, or first prom sat in stunned silence. With varying levels of comprehension, they realized that neither Halloween nor the homecoming dance might come this year, or perhaps ever again. American schools and civil defense agencies had done a comprehensive job of alerting children to the dangers of nuclear war; now perhaps they thought they had done their job too well as World War III seemed to become an imminent possibility.

During the next few days the long-feared nuclear war very nearly happened, and as Soviet ships probed the American naval blockade, CBS anchor Walter Cronkite described a litany of probable moves and countermoves that he strongly hinted would end in war unless miraculously short-circuited. Then, as one Kennedy official noted, Washington and Moscow went "eyeball to eyeball," and the other side "blinked." Children across the nation took cues from their parents and collectively exhaled. Suddenly the failure to study for an upcoming math test would actually (and thankfully) once more have consequences. Now it again mattered whether your mother purchased a Casper the Ghost costume or turned you into a Halloween ghost with homemade materials.

None of the 76 million Boomers would see the cold war end during their childhood or even during their young adulthood. Soon after the Cuban Missile Crisis, the struggle between the United States and Communist powers would push the nation into the war that defined the Boomer generation and produced conflict at home as well as abroad. Yet once those October days had passed, and trick-or-treat and Halloween dances had pushed war fears into the background, the collective near-death experiences of Boomer children gradually returned to activities that would later reignite the nostalgia for Camelot. The United States and the Soviet Union quickly installed a "hot line" communications system that at least made accidental war less likely. In June 1963 the young president, in a dramatic commencement address at American University, emphasized the commonalities, rather than the differences, between the rival powers and set the stage for a nuclear test ban. As young Americans watched their president mobbed by cheering Europeans from Dublin to Berlin, and meeting with leaders who always appeared much older, the link between the young leader and the Boomer generation seemed almost magical.

Children who lived during the Kennedy era experienced a moment in American youth culture that continued to fascinate Boomers far beyond the tragedy of Dallas. Almost as soon as the sixties ended, movie producers enticed patrons with catchphrases such as "Where Were You in '62?" and used the New Frontier era as a backdrop for Catskill dance contests, college food fights, and Baltimore teen rebellion against segregation. Probably 50 million Boomers were old enough to experience the Camelot years on some level, and most of the remaining members of that generation participated indirectly through "Oldies" music, retrospective films, or DVDs of period television series. What they witnessed was a transition in which television, films, popular music, and fashion would ultimately make the Boomers a prime target of attention.

In the early sixties two television programming trends and a significant technological innovation influenced Boomer viewing habits and their interaction with other family members. First, beginning in 1962, the television networks dropped most of their Westerns and filled many of these time slots with programs centered on World War II themes. Program developers who had exploited every conceivable aspect of the frontier experience now treated the recent global conflict from multiple angles. *Combat!*, *The Gallant Men*, and *Twelve O'clock High* focused respectively on the war in France, Italy, and the bomber offensive against Germany. *McHale's Navy* and *Broadside* provided comic views of the

Pacific war, featuring the crew of a PT boat and a detachment of WAVES. *The Rat Patrol* chronicled the North African campaign, and *Garrison's Guerrillas* delivered stories of undercover operations and spies. While historical accuracy and plot development varied enormously, these programs offered Boomer children a new perspective on the wartime experiences of their parents and an opportunity for discussion with them about this defining event. Every character, from the gritty bravery of Sergeant Saunders of *Combat!* to the officious pettiness of Captain Binghamton of *McHale's Navy*, provided a backdrop for family interchange between the "Greatest Generation" and their postwar heirs.

While this trend encouraged Boomers to see recent historical events from their parents' perspective, the other major programming shift emphasized the comic and dramatic aspects of growing up in the 1960s and sparked a different kind of dialogue. Comedies such as *Dobie Gillis* and *Patty Duke* viewed the high school experience through the interactions of teenagers and their parents. *Mr. Novak* added the perspective of an idealistic young English teacher and a somewhat more cynical school principal. *Fair Exchange* offered the intriguing premise of transatlantic comparisons of teenage experiences through young female exchange students.

If both these program concepts offered opportunities to bridge the parent-child divide, a major technological innovation began the move toward more isolated and fragmented viewing habits that are so much a part of twenty-first-century leisure activities. In the fifties most television sets had been bulky and seldom-moved pieces of furniture as much as entertainment appliances. Late in the decade, portable televisions were introduced that could be moved from room to room on a wheeled cart or carried with some difficulty.

In 1963 General Electric introduced a "personal portable" television, essentially an array of tubes encased in a light-weight plastic shell, which weighed about ten pounds and sold for $99. The new sets were colorful, relatively durable, and easily transportable, and quickly became a popular gift to children and teenagers, who could now watch their own choice of programs relatively free of adult supervision or decision-making. Yet the fifties tradition of family television viewing was not immediately broken, and for the near term Boomer kids seemed to slide effortlessly between the larger-screen (and, increasingly) color television in the living room or family room and the privacy of the new portable models.

Just as television viewing habits seemed to straddle two eras during the Kennedy years, the films watched by young people during this era looked backward and forward in their cultural impact. As noted earlier, teen horror and juvenile delinquency films largely peaked in the mid-to-late fifties and then rapidly disappeared in favor of new concepts. On the one hand, the films produced primarily for adolescent or pre-teen audiences in the early sixties demonstrate a trend away from young people as threats to society and more toward mildly comical adventures. This era produced the beginning of the "surf" trend, with teen heartthrobs Sandra Dee and James Darren initiating the *Gidget* series, and Annette Funicello and Frankie Avalon countering with the *Beach Party* series. By this time, switchblades and leather jackets (in black and white) had given way to surfboards and skis (in color) as adults ranging from meddling parents to curious college professors looked on in bemusement at the sometimes incomprehensible antics of the young generation.

While the shift of film teens from gang wars to surfing tournaments was probably a net gain for parental piece of

The southern California youth culture, centered on surfing, cars, and high school sports rivalries, proved to be easily transportable to many parts of America far from an ocean, and made stars of California's Beach Boys. *(Michael Ochs Archives/CORBIS)*

mind, the trend in horror films clearly increased adult concern about influences on their children's behavior. The teen horror films of the fifties had been modestly violent but, in perspective, probably no more violent than the Westerns of that era. By the early sixties young people were temporarily supplanted as the focus of horror, but the plots, still often watched by young audiences, were far more disturbing. Two Alfred Hitchcock films released during the Kennedy era made the earlier teen horror films look mild by comparison and initiated a still controversial trend in youth viewing habits. Hitchcock's 1960 film *Psycho* shocked audiences with its famous "shower scene," in which Janet Leigh's character is slashed to death by a psychotic motel manager played by

Anthony Perkins. While the film attracted far more adult patrons than the teen horror movies, a good many young people viewed this genesis of the "slasher" genre. Three years later Hitchcock added a new dimension with *The Birds*. Filmed in color, it heightened the shock effect, replacing the single slasher scene with repeated bloody confrontations between malevolent birds and largely helpless humans. In one scene youngsters are savagely attacked at a birthday party, in another scene outside their classroom, and an eleven-year-old girl becomes a focal point for the terror as the threat heightens. While neither of these films offered the pessimistic vision of young people depicted in the fifties, their style served as a gateway for the genre that would concern parents and teachers for the foreseeable future.

While a substantial number of television programs and motion pictures were clearly made with a Boomer audience in mind, much of the music industry was also concentrating on young people as its primary customers. Adult music enthusiasts still enjoyed dominance in prime-time television programs such as the *Perry Como Show* and the *Lawrence Welk Show*, and long-playing stereo albums commanded a majority of adult sales until later in the decade. But the targeted audience for the enormously popular "singles" format was now primarily Boomers while the rock-and-roll format preferred by this age group was becoming more sophisticated and sometimes inviting adults to join the fun.

As John Kennedy was settling into the White House, a new music craze was firmly drawing a line between the fifties and the sixties, and persuading more than a few adults that rock music was not as threatening as they initially believed. A few months earlier a young South Philadelphia teenager named Ernest Evans had released a record called

"The Twist" under the name of Chubby Checker. Beyond the catchy music, this new dance released listeners from the rules of couples' or line dancing and essentially made each person on the dance floor a free agent. Dancers on *American Bandstand* quickly adapted to the Twist, and soon very adult nightclubbers at trendy New York venues such as the Peppermint Lounge discovered that this was the first rock-and-roll format that could be adapted to older dancers—a reality made even more exciting by the emergence of women's fashions designed primarily for an evening of carefree Twisting. As this form of early-sixties rock and roll attracted a new, older audience that had previously rejected the music, other new trends solidified the preteen and adolescent Boomer audience that had initially been the target of the novelty tunes and teen idols of the late fifties.

A number of print, television, or motion picture chronicles of the sixties have emphasized the role of the Beatles and other British bands in "rescuing" a dying American popular music scene that had begun to unravel with the death or retirement of numerous rock pioneers. A closer examination of the period reveals that rock and roll had already entered an exciting transformation period by late 1962 or early 1963, fully a year before most Americans had heard of Paul McCartney or John Lennon. Much of the rebirth was the result of Boomers engaged as both consumers and creators of the new music. At least three major formats are evident in 1963, and each would have an important cultural and social impact on Boomer perceptions of their childhood and their environment.

The first trend was the emergence of a more substantial feminine presence in rock and roll in the form of "girl groups," which included both ensembles and individual performers. While fifties teenage girls had bought substantial

Chubby Checker, left, became the first superstar of the sixties when he enticed adults to enter the teenage world of rock and roll through the medium of the "Twist" dance craze. *(Time & Life Pictures/Getty Images)*

numbers of rock-and-roll records, the music was sung almost entirely by male artists. Many hit songs were about girls but mostly concerned the triumph and tragedy of romance from a male perspective. This reality began to change in the early 1960s when a group called the Shirelles made a top hit with the haunting ballad "Will You Love Me Tomorrow?" Quickly building on that success, three young husband-and-wife teams working out of the Brill Building in New York City, and a young male alumnus of a 1950s group working out of Gold Star Studios in Los Angeles, produced a string of records that featured female singers backed by increasingly sophisticated production values.

The three couples, Gerry Geffen and Carole King, Jeff Barry and Ellie Greenwich, and Barry Mann and Cynthia Weil, and the single man, Phil Specter, engaged in friendly competition and lucrative collaborations to produce songs that often defined female Boomer adolescence yet had a pulsing, danceable beat that attracted male listeners. Enlisting female singers from a diversity of African-American, Latino, and white backgrounds, girl groups such as the Crystals, the Ronettes, and the Angels sang about a wide range of emotions, from pride in a nonconformist boyfriend ("He's a Rebel") to frustration with parental interference ("We're Not Too Young to Get Married"), to the magic of meeting a potential life partner ("Today I Met the Boy I'm Going to Marry"). While often dismissed by adult critics as "teen operas," these songs resonated so heavily with Boomer audiences that advertising executives of later decades would use songs like "Be My Baby" and "My Boyfriend's Back" as soundtracks for numerous commercials. The catchy lyrics continued to appeal to listeners who were born long after the original recordings.

While the girl groups were recruited primarily from the Northeast, a parallel but mostly male celebration of Boomer adolescence was growing at the other end of the continent. As the sport of surfing swept California beaches in the early sixties, a surfer-musician named Dick Dale provided an instrumental background to the pounding waves and the foaming sea. By 1962 an aspiring songwriter named Brian Wilson formed a group with his two brothers, a cousin, and a family friend and began to add lyrics to the surfing saga. They called themselves the Beach Boys, and their first album, "Surfin' Safari," became a huge regional hit and a modest national success. In the summer of 1963 follow-up songs "Surfin' USA" and "Surfer Girl" carried the images of the California beach scene to Boomers who had never seen the ocean. Soon vocal duo Jan and Dean's song "Surf City," and instrumentals such as "Wipe Out" and "Pipeline," were hinting that the West Coast, where the suntans of endless summer and the freeways patrolled by fleets of convertibles formed an adolescent paradise, was the single most attractive place in the world to be young.

Midway between Manhattan's Brill Building and Malibu's beach parties, a third new kind of music was rising from the gritty streets of Detroit. Energetic entrepreneur Berry Gordy was spending the Kennedy years fashioning a music empire by forming primarily African-American groups with an appeal that would transcend race among Boomers. By 1963 the distinctive purple record label of Motown Records was a major element in most stocks of 45s as the Miracles' "Mickey's Monkey," Martha and the Vandellas' "Heat Wave," and Stevie Wonder's "Fingertips" became summer anthems. While these songs secured Gordy's place as an enormously successful minority business leader, he was already busy auditioning groups such as the Temptations, the Four Tops, and the Supremes, who would form much of the soundtrack of the rest of the decade.

Thus any Boomer armed with a transistor radio in 1963 was probably unaware that a group of young men from Liverpool would be needed to "rescue" rock and roll from its imminent demise. In fact the Beatles were so excited by the American scene that their early albums consisted primarily of covers of the same songs that later chronicles would dismiss as banal or sterile. Not only were the Boomers excited about "their" music well before the Beatles' arrival, members of their own generation were just now emerging as recognizable performers. By 1963 postwar babies such as Peggy March, Lesley Gore, and Stevie Wonder were piling up strings of hits, and Gore's birthday lament of "It's My

Party" came from an authentic Boomer sixteen-year-old, not a young adult looking back in time.

Many Boomers recall the Kennedy era as a real-life Camelot, punctuated by music, television, and films that chronicled their passage through childhood and adolescence. But at the time, adults of the era, unaware of the looming cultural upheaval, had more mixed reviews of the new generation. A growing number of magazine articles and television specials suggested that these postwar children were growing up before they were ready to handle minimal adult responsibility. In "Boys and Girls Too Old Too Soon," *Life* magazine warned that America's preteens were rushing toward trouble as ten-to-twelve-year-old girls turned themselves out in mascara and high-style hairdos, and boys turned into party hounds. Under pressure to go steady, engaged in constant campaigns to captivate each other or be captured, young boys and girls became involved in subteen romances complete with wraparound dancing and necking. Profiling one twelve-year-old girl, *Life* described her as a "pocket *femme fatale* who can wrap a boy around her little finger and works hard at it." She was considered representative of "a generation whose jumble of innocence and worldly wisdom is unnaturally precocious and alarming."

Interviews with early-sixties preteens revealed that parents often considered the young relationships "cute," or simply allowed themselves to be stampeded by the sheer numbers involved. Some women took their daughters to suburban beauty parlors to keep up with the latest coiffure while other girls routinely spent two hours with friends creating beehive hairdos. The garment industry tapped into this market with "training bras" and small-size garter belts to hold up special small-size stockings. Some newspaper advertisements enticed girls to purchase wigs so that "now you can be as glamorous as mother."

In large families of the period, some parents who had their hands full with babies or toddlers regarded preteen dating as the least of their immediate concerns. In a period of continued low divorce rates, marriage was still viewed as the institution that guaranteed happiness and security to all, especially as it was depicted in movies, television, and romance magazines. Thus some preteens who should have had a person of their age and gender as their best friend often found themselves with a miniature husband or wife. While they needed to belong in groups, pairing often was the necessary ticket of admission to many social functions.

While preteens basked in the ingratiating attention of their "steadies" and talked incessantly on the telephone hashing over the boys and girls in their lives, the Boomers who had become the vanguard of the high school genera-tion in the early sixties were more frequently being noted for their restlessness and anti-social behavior. By the time the high school became the exclusive domain of the postwar baby surge, otherwise peaceful suburban communities tried to cope with teenagers who lacked the black leather jackets and pompadours of the fifties juvenile delinquents but could become equally threatening in khakis and crew cuts.

The summer vacation season became a potential time of trouble as waves of Boomer teens competing for limited summer jobs pushed a growing minority of bored adoles-cents toward gate-crashing, vandalism, and violence. Jour-nalists cited the almost biblical status among teens of books such as *Catcher in the Rye, A Separate Peace,* and *Lord of the Flies*, and noted that an almost tribal atmosphere was developing in the parking lots and booths of suburban restaurants as boys and girls shuttled from car to car and booth to booth with the single greeting, "Where's the party?" As one writer observed, "Almost every high school student in the nation has access to a car, his own, his parents' or that of a friend, while teens evade the liquor laws just as successfully as his father or grandfather dodged the Volstead Act." Critics emphasized that while parents of earlier generations had considered themselves negligent if they did not know the whereabouts of their children at all times, in the sixties a teen could announce, in all honesty, that he was driving over to a friend's house to watch television. He might do so, and yet, before the evening was over, he and his friend, plus others picked up along the way, might visit a drive-in restaurant, a liquor store, look in on two or three parties, and cruise twenty miles on back roads to the music of blaring radios. Unless the teen telephoned home every half-hour, his or her parents would not know the exact location of their son or daughter.

Within a few years such concerns would pale in comparison to the generational confrontations instigated by the Vietnam War and the rising counterculture. By the standards of 1968 or 1969, preteens of 1962 and high school students of 1963 seemed far less threatening and far more integrated into the overall American culture. As the final summer of the Kennedy era drifted from one sun-drenched day to another, and throngs of adoring European citizens mobbed the young president, the Boomers emerged as idols for much of the young population of the planet. American popular music, films, and television spread the nation's ideas and values over the globe. The Boomers were the youngest citizens of a young country that, despite significant challenges, was basically rich, free, and envied. Around the globe, young people of other nations played American records, watched American television and films, spoke American slang, and copied American youth fashions in a yearning to feel, at least vicariously, in touch with their counterparts in the United States. For one last summer season in Camelot, young American boys in chinos, loafers, and madras sport shirts, and young girls in Capri pants or Bermuda shorts, tennis shoes or sandals, defined modernity and youthfulness far beyond their nation's borders. Then, in the words of Nat "King" Cole's last hit that season, those "Hazy, Lazy, Crazy Days of Summer" drew to an inevitable close, and the oldest Boomers entered their senior year of high school with college on the horizon for many. Before their senior year was half finished, the idolized president would be slain, and before their final college exams, Martin Luther King and Robert Kennedy would join John Fitzgerald Kennedy in the pantheon of recent American martyrs.

7

BOOMERS IN TRANSITION: HIGH SCHOOL TO COLLEGE

SOON AFTER Labor Day 1963, the promises and challenges of the great postwar birth surge coalesced in a major milestone. As beaches, campgrounds, and amusement parks became noticeably quiet, the children returning to school from kindergarten to the twelfth grade were, for the first time, all Boomers. Predictions from the forties and fifties that the surge in births would eventually affect every aspect of the public school system had now become reality, and there was no hint that the situation would change in the foreseeable future. One small consolation in this ongoing demographic crisis was that the United States now had a school population that completed the entire sequence of grades up to high school graduation in overwhelming numbers. Thus projections for future enrollments would be accurate enough to plan for faculty and facilities expansion if teachers could be found and funds raised.

Yet in the fall of 1963 the educational establishment, the Boomers, and their parents were about to enter uncharted territory: students had a legal right to education through high school, but they had no such right to higher education. Each public and private institution was relatively free to expand as little or much as it chose, regardless of the needs of the Boomers who were about to seek admission to its campus. As Boomer seniors settled into their twelfth-grade rituals and routines, many faced not only the opportunities and challenges of their final year of traditional public education but also a complex national game of academic musical chairs where the number of college applicants exceeded the seats that could accommodate them. The teenagers who entered the college admissions sweepstakes of the 1960s faced an anxiety level that would never fully be appreciated or duplicated by their descendants in the late twentieth and early twenty-first centuries. The number of applicants was growing faster than colleges were expanding to accommodate them, while the whole process of acceptance and rejection was played against the backdrop of military conscription and the Vietnam War.

For most postwar children the transition from high school to college began as they moved from tenth to eleventh grade. Junior year of high school was the time for the first formal prom, the training course that would lead to a coveted driver's license, and the first career workshops offered by the school guidance staff. Eleventh grade also included one-on-one meetings with counselors who perused transcripts and often bluntly advised whether the child was indeed "college material." Meanwhile "college nights" featured admissions personnel from a variety of schools who sometimes exhibited the smugness of individuals who knew their product was in greater demand than the supply could possibly accommodate.

As the juniors negotiated their way through a curriculum and grading system that had been made much more demanding in the wake of Sputnik, these early Boomers had their first encounter with the imposing bureaucracy of the CEEB, the College Entrance Examination Board. Sometime during the fall of their junior year, millions of teenagers took the PSAT, the Pre-Scholastic Aptitude Test that was a type of preview of the SAT, which was such a crucial factor in the college admissions process. Although counselors assured students that the PSAT did not "count" in any permanent sense, students and parents anxiously awaited the results and did the calculations that would turn the raw score into a rough preview of what might be expected in the "real thing" a few months later.

The closing months of the junior year usually brought the first encounter with the full-fledged "College Boards," including the standard verbal and math examination and the aptitude tests that paralleled course subjects. These scores would usually arrive on a hot summer afternoon in the middle of school vacation, and the results—somewhere between the minimum of 200 and the maximum of 800—might prompt a family conference to help determine where, or if, an early Boomer would rise to the next level of education. On a group level the Boomers of the high school class of 1964 entered the testing season with enormous success. This class achieved the highest SAT scores of any group before or after, and would become the gold standard as scores gradually declined in future decades. Yet individually these children entered their final year of high school competing for college acceptance in a system that was simply not ready for them. Unlike their children, who would be asked by adults, "*Where* are you going to college?" the first Boomers would be asked, "*Did* any college accept you?" Senior year placed these teens in two worlds, a universe of the culminating activities and events of the high school experience, and another world of tense anticipation in which alternate plans were serious possibilities in case the response from every college was the dreaded thin envelope that contained the single sheet of paper signifying rejection.

High school yearbooks of 1964 contain many features that would not look out of place in comparable annuals more than four decades later. Photos and commentary describe a breezy social whirl of homecoming dances, proms, and school plays. Successful athletic teams are held up as beacons of pride while even losing teams "played their hearts out" or gained "moral victories" in close losses. Candid classroom photos show popular teachers and eager students engaged in a more exciting learning process than most students remembered on most class days. A Who's Who section pairs a boy and girl as "Best Dressed," "Most Musical," "Best Looking," "Class Clowns," "Most Popular," or "Most Likely to Succeed." Photos of social events hint at the ever-changing dating universe, where the couples at the fall homecoming dance may or may not be with the same partners at the senior prom.

The centerpiece of a high school yearbook, whether in the 1960s or the twenty-first century, is the section displaying all the graduating seniors, more formally dressed than on most ordinary school days. A litany of activities—Chorus 1, 2, 3, Football 3, 4, or Class President 4—hints at continuing and changing interests and the most popular or least active graduates. Beyond the changing fashion statements and the notes on activities, a difference in yearbooks several decades apart may be seen in the "future plans" under senior photos. A relatively typical twenty-first-century high school yearbook would list nearly three of four seniors intending to continue in school in a wide spectrum of institutions, from community colleges to world-class universities. But for about half the members of the first class of Boomer high school graduates, future plans would include specific jobs, marriage plans, military service, or vague assurances that a particular graduate "will be successful in anything he attempts" or have a "rewarding career in her chosen profession." Many of these Boomers were in their last year of formal education, and more than a few would become parents in the very near future. Many of the cute couples in those yearbook photos were already pricing engagement rings.

The large number of Boomers for whom senior year in high school was probably their last school experience viewed twelfth grade from a different perspective. Many of these teens had found schoolwork a daunting combination of boring and difficult, and were tired of regimentation and bell schedules. They hoped their post-school careers would be more exciting and knew that work was more financially rewarding than school. Boys dreamed of buying their own car, girls thought about dramatically enhanced fashion choices, less encumbered by dress codes. For these students, the last game, the last dance, and the last prom carried greater nostalgia than the last class and the last exam.

The roughly equal number of Boomers who aspired to college viewed their senior year as a different transition. "College preparatory" courses in high school were already demanding, yet counselors, teachers, films, and books suggested that college would be even more daunting, with professors more stern and unyielding than high school teachers. College did offer the prospect of more choice of courses, less adult supervision, and a social life where fraternities, sororities, and related social activities were still a major and well-publicized part of the collegiate lifestyle. But senior year produced a number of decisions and complications. In the early sixties a boy was nearly twice as likely to attend college as a girl, and many high school couples wondered what would happen to their relationship if one went away to college while the other remained at home. Was the school close enough that the person staying home could visit on weekends? Would the student come home relatively often? Should either person be free to explore other relationships? Would an extended engagement be viable?

Boys contemplating college also had to include the prospect of compulsory military service in their plans. Should they enlist and enter college at a more mature age, enter a college ROTC program, seek a major that might secure a draft deferment, or take their chances on being drafted after graduation? Some of these options would be affected by the fact that while draft boards granted draft deferments for full-time students, anyone slipping below a C average for even a semester would be thrown into the draft eligibility pool. As the Vietnam War expanded and casualties rose, these decisions took on still greater importance.

In early June 1964 the oldest Boomers encountered their last round of high school examinations and attended commencement services that offered a bittersweet theme: a nation with seemingly unlimited economic potential, and the traumatic experience of John Kennedy's death partway through the academic year. The New Frontier and Lyndon Johnson's now emerging Great Society had produced generous pay raises, low rates of unemployment, and excellent job prospects for both high school and college graduates. Unlike their parents, this first cohort of Boomers boasted a near 90 percent graduation rate. During that summer at least some teens waiting to enter college must have experienced a twinge of envy for their peers who had already entered the workforce and were showing off their new cars, new clothes, and other short-term advantages over college.

The summer of 1964 emerged as a transitional period not only for the first Boomers but for American society as a whole. While many recent graduates inhabited that limbo between high school and college, the larger nation experienced urban riots, the murder of civil rights workers in the Deep South, a contentious Democratic National Convention in Atlantic City, and an escalation of the simmering Vietnam conflict after the Gulf of Tonkin resolution in Congress. At a few schools, such as the University of California at Berkeley, a confrontational mood spilled over into the first full-fledged campus protest of the sixties, the Free Speech Movement led by Mario Savio. Yet in September new students arrived on the campuses of a nation that was generally upbeat about its future.

A lead feature in an early-autumn edition of one national magazine marveled at the prospects for American society. "An astonishing, unprecedented prosperity pervades the country. The GNP has risen $112 billion in three years. There aren't enough pots to hold the chickens or enough garages to go around. Just as astonishing as the prospect is the way Americans take it for granted."

As anxious and excited Boomers made tearful farewells to parents and siblings, an entire nation seemed vicariously to follow the exploits of the Spock babies who had now reached late adolescence. In some respects their college rituals would seem strikingly familiar to students inhabiting twenty-first-century universities. The endless trek with boxes and parcels from the spacious family car to a less than spacious dorm room; the initial exchanges between roommates who would now become major figures in one another's lives; the alternately serious and silly rituals of freshman orientation; and the experience of sitting in a college lecture hall dominated by an erudite yet intimidating professor are hallmarks of both eras.

Beyond these commonalities, the collegiate world of 1964 would seem positively quaint nearly a half-century later. While the freshman world of 1964 would be seen as relatively casual compared to other generations of collegians, blazers and ties for men, skirts and dresses for women were still essential parts of a campus wardrobe. Students wearing flip-flops, shorts, and hooded sweatshirts would probably receive an invitation from the instructor to leave the classroom.

Residence life, that part of the "college experience" that now seems so important that counselors and parents encourage dormitory life for students who have a family home five miles from campus, was both less pervasive and yet far more regulated when the Boomers entered college. On the one hand, many urban institutions of the early sixties saw their mission as augmenting classroom space rather than dormitory space to meet the Boomer surge; in turn, many parents of college students who themselves had not attended college saw residence life as slightly absurd if their sons or daughters could easily take a subway, bus, or car to class and live free at home. Major urban universities, such as City College of New York, UCLA, the University of Wisconsin at Milwaukee, Villanova, and Loyola of Chicago, were typical city schools that concentrated on the instruction of large numbers of commuters, with dormitory space limited to students attending from long distances.

One of the realities of college life in 1964 that made commuters less inclined to envy their dormitory counterparts was that in many cases residence life was both more spartan and stricter than accommodations at home. American colleges had never been known for providing sumptuous housing, and since most sixties institutions were overcrowded, comfortable residence halls were often at a premium. Dormitories might include old structures beyond their prime, semi-permanent buildings slapped together to handle the G.I. Bill surge of veterans, and new facilities designed to hold maximum numbers of students. The combination of outdated or subpar electrical outlets and a general desire to discourage students from wasting time encouraged many colleges to forbid private television sets or telephones in rooms. Television viewing often became a communal experience as students sprawled around dormitory lounges where either the majority or the most vocal students determined choice of programs. Telephone use was often another form of communal enterprise as students queued to make calls as other residents hovered impatiently for their turn. Incoming calls largely depended on someone in the hall bothering to answer the phone or convey the message to the intended party.

If dormitories provided few choices for entertainment, dining halls offered equally few selections. A society in which few children were asked their preference for dinner at home was consistent in its attitude toward students "away at college." Most meals offered one main course, though substitutions might be permitted. College dining services were also split between schools that allowed students to take multiple helpings and those that limited diners to one serving, forcing many students to rely on dorm snack machines for extra calories.

Communal phones and limited meal selections tended to be secondary concerns in the greater conflict between the individual and the university over the right of decision-making and autonomy. The first Boomers entered college at a time when the recent domination of university life by the "Silent Generation" of the 1950s had lulled administrators into a belief that the major crisis of the new decade would be swelling numbers, not serious student rebellion. *In loco parentis* was still taken quite seriously in the colleges of 1964 as student curfews and gender separation in residence facilities sometimes offered a student less freedom than he or she experienced at home. The relatively arbitrary rules and sanctions that permeated the college experience for the arriving postwar generation were particularly frustrating when they were linked to the daunting academic grind of the mid-sixties.

The demographic backdrop to the arrival of the Boomers was the stark reality that the 2.7 million college students of 1950 were now the 4.8 million of 1964, and that number was soaring with a baby boom that had not yet ended. A Yale freshman complained to an interviewer, "I feel like a mail-order bride as the work is poured on much faster than I expected and my teachers calmly refer to 'those who stay in this course'; many of us are putting in 18-hour days to compete for a 'C' average." Many very good high school students experienced their first taste of failure as reality came crashing down on them. More than a few teachers were encouraged by their superiors to grade on a strict curve, which guaranteed a substantial number of Ds and Fs. Some

While Boomer college students of the mid-sixties began to challenge some traditions and rules, many aspects of the college experience were relatively slow to change. (Getty Images)

instructors graded more harshly, which could produce a class in which more than half of the enrolled students failed. This process produced a steady, barely subdued feeling of panic as students put in all the hours they could and still received grades that placed them on the brink of dismissal. Students agonized over the embarrassment of devolving from the high school "brain" to a dismissed college freshman returning home in disgrace. Even students with passable grades complained that on good nights they were able to sleep fewer than six hours while on some nights there was no sleep at all.

A Yale dean admitted that the high school class of 1964 faced "shattering pressure as their academic world tumbles down on them. They only accept it because they know everybody else is in the same boat." Students frequently admitted to guilt feelings when they took even one night off from studying, and by the end of the fall term more than 20 percent required psychological counseling, even if they had escaped the dreaded letter of dismissal. Boomer students were thrust into a far more demanding environment than earlier collegians as colleges reluctantly accepted more students than they could possibly house or instruct and then employed a draconian grading policy to shrink the class to more manageable levels.

One of the results of this intellectual component to cold-war competition was a sense of uncertainty, anxiety, and fear of failure, from freshman student to college president. Media narratives and photographs of the period are filled with poignant images of dismissed students packing their books and saying goodbye to roommates while hurrying out of the dorm before the tears came. In other images, shocked and disbelieving parents usher their child toward the family station wagon, no doubt wondering how to tell friends and neighbors that their high school star has become a collegiate academic failure.

On a higher level, many of the Boomers' professors found themselves caught between a rapidly escalating emphasis on publishing and a rapidly expanding pool of students who wanted instruction and advice. Even in an environment where colleges were hiring five new instructors for every faculty member who retired, professors still greatly feared a downward career spiral, in which failure to publish sufficiently might result in a move to a lesser school in "academic Siberia," and poor student feedback might bring the same fate.

Finally, college presidents agonized over the approval of desperately needed expansion projects before financing had been completed, and raided other schools for faculty while attempting to foil raids against their own institutions. College executives who only a few years earlier had worried about smaller enrollments than expected now spent most of their waking hours dealing with the needs of a new generation whose numbers could barely be accommodated.

Even before Boomers were exposed to the social ferment of the campus of the late sixties, these students could see an era of change coming that would make their collegiate experience different from that of their older siblings. Yet the face of this change varied substantially across the range of the higher-education spectrum.

One of the most significant instructional developments in the period was directly related to the surge in student numbers. As colleges searched for new instructors to meet the growing need, graduate students were increasingly pressed into service as teaching fellows and teaching assistants. While many of them were young and energetic, they were also still students who had to manage their own assignments and examinations. Thus they often viewed their teaching duties as an imposition on their time. Also, a growing number of assistants and fellows in the sciences and mathematics were arriving in the United States from foreign nations with excellent minds but poor English-language skills, which made for torturous instruction in classes where concepts and facts were difficult to understand in perfect English. As class sizes grew and senior faculty avoided undergraduate classes in favor of research and doctoral seminars, more than a few students experienced the depersonalized atmosphere of huge lecture halls in which classes were taught by distracted, distant professors, with examinations graded by mechanical devices.

The gender makeup of classes was just beginning to change in a number of universities and colleges. Unlike early-twenty-first-century students who enter a higher education system where only 1 percent of institutions are open to a single gender, the Boomers entered college when nearly half of private schools were single-sex institutions and coeducation was still spotty and erratic at numerous public institutions. In 1964, for example, six of the eight Ivy League schools accepted only male undergraduates. The University of Pennsylvania featured coeducational classes with separately administered colleges for men and women, and only Cornell University accepted women with no restrictions. Outstanding female students who desired an Ivy education outside of Penn or Cornell could opt for "coordinate" women's colleges such as Radcliffe (Harvard), Pembroke (Brown), or Barnard (Columbia), or attend other "Seven Sister" schools such as Mount Holyoke, Bryn Mawr, and Vassar. Prominent Catholic universities, such as Notre Dame, Georgetown, and Villanova, were either exclusively male or allowed women into only a handful of majors. Villanova enrolled five thousand men in its Arts, Sciences, Business, and Engineering colleges while two hundred women enrolled in the School of Nursing were allowed to enroll in English, history, and science courses limited to their gender. Even some state universities separated men and women whenever possible. While the University of North Carolina at Chapel Hill was open primarily to undergraduate males, females were expected to attend the Greensboro campus, which was essentially a women's college. The state of Florida was in the process of making both the University of Florida, formerly a men's school, and Florida State University, a women's school, into coeducational institutions, with emphasis on the budding sports rivalry just beginning to develop at the two schools.

Students attending the majority of colleges that were co-educational by the mid-sixties discovered that differences in career goals continued to create classes that were dominated by one gender. Pennsylvania's flagship state school, Penn State, featured extensive programs in agriculture, mining, engineering, and business, which produced a campus where males outnumbered females by more than two to one. On the other hand, the commonwealth's fourteen "state teachers' colleges" focused on elementary education, library science, and home economics, which guaranteed a heavily female student population. While girls were already beginning to dominate high school honor societies and honor rolls, they were entering college at a time when selecting a major outside traditional fields such as nursing, education, or home economics was still something of an adventure. Yet by 1964 the career "rules" were no longer etched in stone, and walls of gender separation were just beginning to crumble in school and workplace.

As gender roles changed, so did social relationships, even if that trend was not fully noticeable early in the Boomer college experience. Unlike the somewhat amorphous and shifting social patterns of twenty-first-century universities, where "hanging out" and "hooking up" carry different meanings for different situations, the first Boomers entered a college environment where most students were actively seeking opposite-sex partners and at least tacitly auditioning candidates for marriage and family formation.

Coeducational colleges offered numerous opportunities to form dating relationships through common classes, university or club social events, and joint social functions sponsored by men's and women's dormitories. At many schools fraternities and sororities were quite active. The 1970s film *Animal House*, which is set in 1962, offers a reasonable if exaggerated approximation of the fraternity system in place when the Boomers arrived at college.

While Greek organizations could be welcoming for students who successfully navigated the rush system, and provided a ready pool of potential boyfriends or girlfriends, there were generally not enough openings to accommodate all the students interested in auditioning for membership. Thus students on some campuses were forced into a potentially demeaning "independent" status, which forced them to craft a social life largely as outsiders, since the all-welcoming Delta House in the film was generally not an option on the real campus of the time.

The large minority of students attending single-sex colleges faced a more daunting task: attempting to meet appealing partners during a finite number of social encounters. Virtually every single-sex college sponsored "mixers," in which bands, refreshments, and dancing attracted members of the opposite sex to come to the school for the evening. Even most rural colleges had a counterpart institution of the other gender within a reasonable distance, and, when necessary, buses could be dispatched to transport guests. One relatively remote New Jersey women's college offered students from men's schools free hors d'oeuvres, dinner in the college's baronial dining hall, and a free admission to the dance to compensate visitors for the distance traveled. Men's colleges in urban areas sponsored mixers that attracted not only female college students but similarly aged "working girls" who had entered careers after high school and often found the prospect of meeting a "college man" an exciting idea.

The mixer scene produced large numbers of budding relationships, but the somewhat forced, formal nature of the process could be less rewarding than the more informal relationships developed by lab partners or study group members in a coed school. And couples enrolled at two different schools could experience long periods without physical companionship and frequent phone calls on erratic dorm phone systems that offered little or no privacy. In some respects, Boomer students who attended single-sex schools in rural areas found their social lives lagging far behind those of high school classmates who had opted for the workaday world and were now developing relationships much more rapidly than their "luckier" college counterparts.

The Boomers who entered college and made the transition from secondary school to higher education without academic dismissal or major psychological trauma were now enrolled in institutions poised for massive change during their college careers. Since the end of Camelot in their senior year of high school, a new president, an expanding war in Vietnam, and new versions of social consciousness were pushing colleges and college students into an unexplored world of change and confrontation. Yet if this new Great Society produced unanticipated challenges, it also dramatically affected children's lives in a wide range of ways, from enhanced educational opportunities to the exuberance of Beatlemania.

\\||//

8

GROWING UP
IN THE GREAT SOCIETY

ON NOVEMBER 22, 1963, John F. Kennedy became immortal, not just for what he had done in life but for what he stood for in death—an unfulfilled dream of a prosperous, confident, envied America moving toward the last third of the twentieth century and the new millennium. The first Boomers would link themselves in a special way to that dream as the president died in their own year of transition from high school to college or career. Yet far more postwar children would be affected by the fact that the stature of the slain president allowed his successor to initiate a new dream that in one way or another touched almost every young person in the nation.

Five days after the fatal shots were fired in Dallas, a somber Texan stood behind the lectern of the House of Representatives and observed that "the greatest leader of our time has been struck down by the foulest deed of our times. All I have I would have given gladly not to be standing here today." Yet now Lyndon Baines Johnson was president of the

United States, and after the shock of his predecessor's death had begun to fade, he found the energy to declare, "Now the ideas and ideal which he [Kennedy] so nobly represented must and will be translated into effective action." Soon this former elementary and high school teacher would propose the legislation necessary to implement a "Great Society" that would affect the lives of all 76 million Boomers. As politicians debated a flurry of bills and community leaders named airports, stadiums, and schools for the slain leader, young Americans passed the mantle of charismatic celebrity from John Kennedy to four young Englishmen.

On Friday, February 7, 1964, Pan Am Flight 101 landed at recently renamed John F. Kennedy Airport in New York, and four modishly dressed young men almost scampered down the aircraft steps as security personnel barely held back thousands of screaming fans, most of whom had skipped school to see Paul McCartney, John Lennon, George Harrison, and Ringo Starr officially launch a British invasion of American youth culture. Two days later a live audience of several hundred bemused adults and ecstatic teens and preteens, and a television audience of 73 million, watched a stiff but cordial welcome by host Ed Sullivan as the Beatles played the first of five songs. Between the first chords of "All My Loving" and the final crescendo of "I Want to Hold Your Hand" nearly an hour later, the younger members of the live audience and their counterparts at home endured Fred Kaps's magic tricks, Frank Gorshin's impressions of Hollywood stars, and Tessie O'Shea's medley of Broadway tunes in order to bask in just under fifteen minutes of performance by four mop-headed Liverpudlians who would quickly entrance nearly every Boomer over the age of five. Within days of their third appearance on Ed Sullivan, the

Beatles would hold the top-four-selling songs and provide a musical beachhead for dozens of other British groups who would take America by storm.

It is impossible to overstate the impact the Beatles and other British acts had on almost any Boomer old enough to enjoy music. If the vigor and magic of the Kennedy presidency defined much of youth culture in the early sixties, Beatlemania became a focal point for Boomers in the middle of this tumultuous decade. Beyond Beatles songs, concerts, movies, and television appearances, the British invasion encouraged more than a few boys to grow their hair longer and adopt at least some elements of British youth fashion while a growing number of American girls looked to London for "smashing" styles and hairdos that changed the appearance of much of young America.

As Boomers lined up outside theaters in the summer of 1964 to watch the Beatles cavort in their first film, *A Hard Day's Night*, President Johnson was energetically transforming the promise of Kennedy's New Frontier into the reality of the Great Society. Almost a year earlier, some 250,000 marchers, perhaps 60,000 of them white, had descended on the sultry national capital to join in peaceful witness to the cause of civil rights. The voice that captured their attention belonged to Martin Luther King, Jr. This was the first time that most Americans had watched King deliver a full-length address, and in many respects his words that day were directed at the emerging Boomer generation, which would dominate the future America of his dream. His initial remarks about the manacles of segregation, the poverty of African Americans, and the horrors of police brutality quickly gave way to a dream of a new beginning "where sons of former slaves and the sons of former slave owners will be able to sit down at the table of brotherhood." At that moment King offered the nation a vision in which the spirit of brotherhood would eventually heal the wounds of racism and slavery, and many of the expectant participants in this future vision were young people watching the drama unfold on flickering television sets on this hot, late-summer afternoon.

A short distance from the site of the demonstration, John Kennedy had watched King's address on television and gradually moved toward support of a civil rights bill that seemed trapped in limbo on the day of the president's assassination. That afternoon, as the tragic events unfolded in Dallas, Martin Luther King's six-year-old son Marty asked innocently, "Daddy, President Kennedy was your best friend, wasn't he?" Almost immediately Lyndon Johnson took up the slain president's goals while using his powerful persuasive talents to push a far more comprehensive list of social reforms.

The foundation of the Great Society was the passage of the most sweeping civil rights legislation since Reconstruction. When opponents of the Civil Rights Act tried to delete critical provisions, Johnson refused to compromise, and before school reopened in the late summer of 1964 the president was able to turn his energies to the goal he most cherished, a massive expansion of educational opportunities for the nation's young people. Johnson, once a passionate, energetic teacher who enjoyed positive results from his imaginative teaching strategies, was now extending his classroom across a continent.

He had been thrust into the presidency of a nation with a massively overcrowded school system in which the five richest states outspent the five poorest states by two to one.

Less than a third of the nation's elementary schools provided a full-fledged library for their pupils, and even those that did frequently had more students than books. Many schools were short of textbooks, scientific equipment, and physical education facilities seven years after the shock of Sputnik had promised massive reform. The president was deeply aware of these problems and insisted that "nothing matters more to the future of our country. The nation's strength, economic productivity, and democratic freedoms all depend on an educated citizenry."

Johnson had watched his predecessor's educational funding bills founder on arguments over equivalent benefits for parochial schools. Now he asked his trusted advisers to create a legislative strategy that would break the impasse. The solution that emerged was to shift the focus of aid to nonpublic schools from the institution to the student. Thus parochial and private students could receive remedial reading instruction, diagnostic testing, counseling services, and many other programs operated out of annexes located just outside the front door of the school, beyond the "wall of separation." Administrators also suggested that school buses, school nurses, and similar provisions were health and safety issues for the individual child and were not direct benefits to the institution. These flexible interpretations transformed many of Kennedy's legislative opponents into supporters of Great Society education bills, and the results were startling.

On Palm Sunday, April 11, 1965, Lyndon Johnson sat on the lawn of his old grade school, Junction Elementary, in New Stonewall, Texas, with his first-grade teacher, Kate Loney, and several of his own former students and signed into law the Elementary and Secondary Education Act of 1965. Six months later the president traveled to his college alma mater, Southwest Texas State University, and put his signature on the Higher Education Act of 1965. In two strokes of a pen the educational opportunities available to the Boomer generation were radically enhanced. The bills served as umbrellas for almost sixty other laws aiding education from preschool through postdoctoral studies.

One of the most innovative programs of the Elementary and Secondary Education Act, which would affect many younger Boomers, was Operation Head Start. This program offered instruction, nutritious meals, counseling, and recreation for disadvantaged preschoolers. It was based on the belief that the environment of poverty created cultural deficits that damaged children's learning, and that it was possible to compensate for these deficits by early intervention in the child's life.

The people involved in Head Start tended to subscribe to the "whole child" concept favored by progressive educators, in which an appropriate education encompassed all the needs and interests of children—emotional, physical, and cultural, as well as academic. For them it was more important to nurture children in a secure environment and to develop learning readiness than to emphasize early attention to academic basics. Thus Head Start programs embraced a wide range of objectives, including motor skill development, advice on family parenting skills, and health and nutrition issues. Within weeks of its inauguration, Head Start enrolled more than a half-million children and received information from hundreds of advisory boards of parents.

Although Head Start was the most rapidly implemented aspect of the Elementary and Secondary Education Act, Boomer children and their parents quickly noticed other changes in their school experience. Elementary schools

One of the most important elements of Lyndon Johnson's Great Society was major educational funding. The president's wife, Lady Bird Johnson, reads to a classroom for Project Head Start, one of the longest-lasting and most influential programs of the Johnson presidency. *(Lyndon Baines Johnson Library)*

that had never operated a library now had funding to hire a school librarian who offered reading awareness programs and ordered substantial numbers of books and related materials under increasingly generous budgets. School counselors, previously limited largely to secondary school vocational interests and college admissions duties, now became involved in more extensive aspects of student life down to the lowest grade levels. University graduate admissions programs found themselves scrambling to find faculty who could instruct future guidance counselors as their numbers seemed to grow geometrically.

The companion Higher Education Act was designed to help colleges cope with the surge of students that had reached six million at the passage of the act and would climb to ten million before current high school freshmen reached their senior year of college. Johnson administration policy-makers were particularly concerned that while 78 percent of high school graduates with a family income over $12,000 now entered college, only 33 percent of those with family income under $3,000 did so. An average mid-sixties family with an income of $6,000 could expect a tuition bill of about $1,500 at a public university and $2,300 at a private college, guaranteeing that only a mortgage payment would produce a larger drain on family income. Great Society legislation now allowed any full-time student to borrow $1,500 a year with no payments until a year after graduation, while Title IV of the Higher Education Act provided an initial $70 million a year in grants of $1,000 to $1,500 a year to lower-income students, coupled with an additional $200 million a year in work-study funds to meet gaps between grants and actual expenses.

The unanimous Senate vote for the Higher Education Act reflected the realization that American higher education was becoming a major element in the ongoing cold-war struggle against the Soviet Union and China, and that virtually every state in the Union could benefit from a massive infusion of federal funds for colleges. Beyond the reality that federal funds would now pay a substantial portion of student tuition, the act also provided both private and public institutions with generous subsidies. For example, Title I budgeted $50 million a year to colleges to study solutions to local community problems; Title II budgeted the same amount for expanding college library acquisitions as well as an additional $415 million to train librarians; Title III offered $55 million a year for teaching fellowships for graduate students and junior faculty to acquire doctorates and gain full faculty status; Title VI provided $275 million a year to the National Teacher Corps to train teachers for low-income school districts; Title VII disbursed $190 million annually to build campus science, mathematics, foreign-language, and engineering facilities.

The enactment of more than sixty laws aiding education could sometimes prove to be a mixed blessing for schools and colleges, where administrators had to cope with an often bewildering mountain of federal regulations and forms. But for most Boomers the Great Society provided enormous benefits, from access to far more books in elementary school libraries to better high school counseling facilities to an opportunity to enter college, even if family income could not support the venture.

Beyond the educational arena, by the mid-sixties the influence of British youth culture on the Boomer generation extended well beyond the initial attraction of the Beatles. At the same time the emergence of color television, cable, and Ultra High Frequency broadcasting dramatically expanded home entertainment horizons, and the rise of James Bond and other related spy films offered Boomers a sophisticated, scary, yet entertaining view of the cold war that so dominated their lives.

The first hint of the distinctiveness of the mid-sixties youth culture came when Boomers surged into theaters to watch a low-budget British black-and-white movie that featured only the sketchiest of plots. *A Hard Day's Night* was essentially a platform for a compilation of new Beatles songs, interspersed with sight gags and a dialogue with such heavy British accents that subtitles would not have been out of place. Watching John, Paul, George, and Ringo romp and sing, millions of young people convinced themselves—and adult America—that the Beatles were not fads that would go the way of Davy Crockett caps and Hula Hoops but represented a freshness and humor that would require mainstream society to sit up and take notice. The television networks quickly got the message that young people now wanted their music to be more than a listening experience. ABC dropped its exuberant, high-rated folk-song program *Hootenanny* for the even more exuberant rock program *Shindig*. NBC followed suit with its own presentation of *Hullaballoo*. Both of these programs featured lithesome, white-booted "go-go" dancers, a live audience of screaming kids, and segments "direct from London" with groups and singers who hoped to make their own transatlantic leap to fame like the Beatles.

Largely due to heavy television promotion and extensive airplay, the Beatles found their monopoly on American attention very short-lived. Although many cynical adults claimed that virtually all of the "British Invasion" acts looked alike and sang alike, each act had a distinctive persona and became a favorite of particular groups of American youngsters. It was soon apparent that the chief threat to the Beatles' supremacy would be the London-based Rolling Stones, whose leaders, Mick Jagger and Brian Jones, presented a grittier, blues-oriented sound and edgier appearance than their Liverpool counterparts. As the Beatles gradually shifted from concert performers and movie stars to a studio experience, the Rolling Stones emerged as the long-term kings of the live performance well into the twenty-first century.

Yet the niches extended far beyond Liverpool versus London. The Kinks featured a driving guitar beat and socially satiric songs that spoke of the frequent boredom of suburban youth on both sides of the Atlantic. The Moody Blues experimented with a fusion of pop-rock and classical.

Herman's Hermits featured incredibly youthful-looking teen singer Peter Noone and lighthearted songs that mesmerized younger audiences while offering American adults a hint of the traditional British music hall experience with hits like "I'm Henry the Eighth." Dusty Springfield used her rather exotic makeup and short skirts to invite American teenage girls into a sophisticated world of romance.

By the close of 1965 American kids could listen to British groups with American names, such as the Dakotas, the Nashville Teens, and the Swinging Blue Jeans; experience the sounds of vaguely scary acts such as the Zombies, the Mindbenders, and the Animals; and even begin to distinguish between the Liverpool accents of Gerry and the Pacemakers and the London accents of the Dave Clark Five. British terms such as "fab" began to replace the American equivalent "boss," and the "mod" fashions of London's Carnaby Street edged into American department stores. As boys' crew cuts gave way to more moppish hairstyles and girls dabbled with the heavy eye makeup and shorter skirts of British "birds," the first hints of a new generation gap emerged between parents and children. Soon these points of contention would seem trivial in comparison to the confrontations of the last years of the decade.

The songs and fashions of the "British Invasion" may have given younger Americans a more sophisticated view of an increasingly international youth culture, but the emergence of a new British film genre hinted that the cold war might be far more complex than they had been taught. In 1963 United Artists released *Dr. No*, the first film version of the British writer Ian Fleming's James Bond novels, which were particular favorites of President Kennedy. The initial film and its sequel, *From Russia with Love*, were solid if not spectacular hits, but in 1964 the even faster action and gadgetry of *Goldfinger* hit the screen in the wake of Beatlemania. Its characters, such as the Korean butler-assassin Odd Job and the female villain-turned-heroine Pussy Galore, suddenly became household names while the largely implied rather than explicit sexual content persuaded more than a few parents tacitly to allow their children to see the film. *Goldfinger* and its two immediate successors, *Thunderball* and *You Only Live Twice*, exposed American young people to a conflict that questioned some of the political realities of both their parents' World War II and the current cold war. In these films, for example, the Soviet Union and its government are virtually never the nemesis to Western security or world peace. At times Russia is depicted as an implicit ally of the West against the far more evil forces of the mysterious renegade organization Spectre, which successively attempts to set off an atomic bomb in Fort Knox, launch a nuclear attack on Miami, and initiate World War III by forcing America and Russia into a confrontation that neither side really wants. In *You Only Live Twice*, the Japanese enemy of only two decades earlier is now depicted as a staunch ally of the West with noble, English-speaking officials commanding fearsome but heroic troops. Each of these films offered the intriguing possibility of a future American-Soviet alliance, with a hint that the cold war was far less pervasive or permanent than children had learned in school.

The huge success of the Bond series quickly influenced the television programs that young viewers found attractive. One of the most popular Bond spinoffs was NBC's *Man from U.N.C.L.E.*, which pitted a UN-like force of agents against a criminal outlaw conspiracy called Thrush. The two top U.N.C.L.E. agents are an American and a citizen of Soviet

Georgia, played by David McCallum, who became the more popular character to young viewers. The spy mania of the mid-sixties also induced NBC to launch the groundbreaking *I Spy*, which paired a white agent, played by Robert Culp, and an African-American operative, played by Bill Cosby, in a series of global adventures largely filmed on location. Cosby became the first black star of a prime-time dramatic series, and the humorous yet socially equal bonding between the two characters became a hopeful sign of changing racial attitudes.

Aside from the action and adventure of numerous spy series, a combination of fantasy, comedy-horror, and science fiction became the subject of numerous cafeteria and after-school conversations. A quintet of comedies featuring comic relations between witches, aliens, genies, and more normal humans attracted even the youngest children. *The Addams Family, The Munsters, Bewitched, My Favorite Martian*, and *I Dream of Jeannie* took lighthearted and occasionally satiric views of situations that in earlier eras had produced terror. Samantha Stevens turned the witch as hag into a glamorous, caring housewife while Tim O'Hara's Martian "Uncle Martin" turned the alien invader persona into a social-life counselor with extraordinary but often comic powers.

The more serious side of this genre emerged with the premiere of *Star Trek* in September 1966, and offered young viewers the tantalizing prospect of an interracial, even interspecies, crew and a basically optimistic view of the world that Boomer descendants would inherit. Most of the crew of the USS *Enterprise* seemed only slightly older than the Boomer viewers, and the plots frequently pitted the impetuous, youthful energy of Captain Kirk against the calm, logical wisdom of Mr. Spock, producing different yet complementary role models. Even young children thrilling to the threats posed by a Salt Creature or Klingon could not help but gain a sense that living in a rapidly changing yet essentially tolerant society was not an unfavorable experience for their own future.

The music, film, and television of the mid-sixties each, in their own way, contributed to a youth culture that challenged Boomers to believe change was good and at least some of the realities of the early postwar world might be challenged. The Great Society offered affluence, increasing educational opportunity, and hope for a more equitable society as Boomers approached adulthood. Yet the Johnson administration's policies in Southeast Asia, the increasingly impersonal and overcrowded atmosphere of the American higher education system, and an emerging generational confrontation over the definition of acceptable personal behavior were all encouraging a fortunate young generation to question the system its elders had constructed.

9

CHALLENGING
THE ESTABLISHMENT

ONLY DAYS before the United States entered the decade that
was to be the Soaring Sixties, Clark Kerr, president of the
burgeoning University of California, appraised the students
who would be attending college over the next decade: "The
employers will love them. They aren't going to press many
grievances. They are going to be easy to handle. There aren't
going to be any riots." Three thousand miles to the east, as
Kerr offered his prediction, four of these "easy to handle"
students were preparing the opening shot of the sixties confrontation between students and the American establishment. Ezell Blair, Franklin McCain, Joseph McNeil, and
David Richmond were freshmen at North Carolina A&T,
an all-black college in Greensboro, North Carolina. They
were attending school in a community with relatively good
educational facilities for minority pupils and were welcome
to spend their money in the city's large Woolworth's department store. But while white customers could relax from
their shopping by enjoying a snack or meal at the store's

lunch counter, this foursome and other members of their race were excluded from that service. On February 1, 1960, the students left campus, headed downtown, sat down at the counter, and ordered coffee. As an astonished policeman paced behind them with no clue how to react, a few white customers cursed the students while others simply shrugged and continued shopping. A few white women even encouraged them, though the students returned to campus without their coffee. Back at school, everyone from the college dean to the student body treated them as heroes. The president of the college asked them why they had even wanted service at a counter with a reputation for tasteless food. The next day more than a dozen classmates joined them at the counter; two days later the first white student participated in the great lunch-counter sit-in while the protest idea spread outward to Durham and Winston-Salem. By Valentine's Day college students in communities from Florida to Tennessee were crowding segregated department store lunch counters amid growing national media attention.

One of the largest and best-organized lunch-counter sit-ins emerged in Nashville and included Fisk University student and later civil rights leader and legislator John Lewis. As Lewis noted, "We had on that first day over five hundred students in front of Fisk University chapel to be transported downtown to the First Baptist Church, to be organized into small groups to go down to sit in at the lunch counters.

"We went into the five-and-tens, Woolworth's, Kresge's, and McClellan's, because these stores were known all across the South and for the most part all across the country. We took our seats in a very orderly, peaceful fashion. The students were dressed like they were on their way to church or going to a big social affair. They had their books, and we

Only a few weeks after the beginning of the 1960s, students at North Carolina A&T sat in at a Woolworth's lunch counter and demonstrated the impact of nonviolent protest against the Establishment. *(Jack Moebes/CORBIS)*

stayed there at the lunch counter, studying and preparing our homework, because we were denied service. The managers ordered that the lunch counters be closed, that the restaurants be closed, and we'd just sit there, all day long."

By mid-April seventy-eight cities in Southern and border states had become part of the sit-in movement. Fifty thousand black students and white sympathizers had participated, enduring anything from sheer boredom to vicious attacks by largely young, white townspeople. Two thousand protesters, including Lewis, were arrested as Northern counterparts threw up picket lines around stores operated by chains that were discriminating in the South. Then, as protesters confronted Nashville mayor Ben West on the steps of city hall, he admitted that discrimination at lunch counters was wrong, and six Nashville counters began serving minority customers in response.

Those first sit-ins of the sixties were organized chiefly by college students who were among the older siblings of the postwar generation. But Boomers would soon be involved in the civil rights movement, and a few of them would not even live to see college. The success of the lunch-counter sit-ins encouraged Martin Luther King to utilize nonviolent protest to end the segregation of public facilities in those parts of the Deep South where the lunch-counter campaign had made little or no impact. In 1963 Birmingham, Alabama, became the battleground in a Children's Crusade pitting Public Safety Director Eugene "Bull" Connor, and his attack dogs and fire hoses, against Boomer teens and children as young as six.

Birmingham in 1963 was one of the most segregated cities in America with "Colored" signs over water fountains, no black police or firefighters, and a chief of public safety who had already orchestrated brutal attacks on so-called Freedom Riders attempting to integrate transportation facilities. Early in the year the jails were filling with adult demonstrators, including Dr. King, in a community that was running out of money to pay their bail. Reverend James Bevel, a veteran of the Nashville sit-ins, suggested massing huge numbers of high school students who could put pressure on the city with less of an economic threat to families if they were arrested as their parents would still be on the job. As Bevel noted, "We started organizing the prom queens of the high school, the basketball stars, the football stars, to get the influence and power leaders involved. They, in turn, got all the other students involved. The students had a community they'd been in since elementary school, so they had bonded

While civil rights demonstrations were planned as peaceful protests, official response was often violent. Television images of vicious dogs attacking protesters, including children, greatly increased white sympathy for civil rights goals. *(Library of Congress)*

quite well. So if one would go to jail, that had a direct effect upon another because they were classmates."

These Boomer teens were given workshops to help them overcome the fear of Bull Connor's canine assault force and the possibility of jail life. Then they began recruiting their elementary-school-age siblings and neighbors, arguing that "Six days in Jefferson County Jail is more educational than six months in our segregated Birmingham schools." May 2, 1963, was dubbed D-Day. As 959 six- to eight-year-old children walked out of the Sixteenth Street Baptist Church, Connor unleashed the dogs and fire hoses. Some of the firefighters used tripod-mounted water cannons designed to fight fires at long range with the power to knock bricks out of a wall from a hundred feet away. As small children rolled down the street under the force of this aquatic artillery, national television cameras recorded the stunning violence for evening news programs. The next day another thousand children were mobilized in the church, and Connor responded with even more attack dogs and fire hoses powerful enough to rip the bark off trees. By nightfall, city jails were filled with nearly two thousand children, and much of the nation watched in disgust as Bull Connor ensured his place in the rogues' gallery of American folklore.

These images of unprovoked and vicious assaults on children apparently sickened President Kennedy too. His staff members organized a temporary truce in which Birmingham stores would be desegregated in exchange for a halt to the protest marches. But hard-core segregationists set off a bombing campaign that included extensive damage to the motel in which Martin Luther King was staying. Then, on September 15, 1963, eighteen days after the March on Washington, the bombers struck again. On a peaceful Sunday the Sixteenth Street Baptist Church was nearly demolished by a powerful explosion. Four young girls, Denise McNair, Carole Robertson, Addie Mae Collins, and Cynthia Wesley, had just finished a Sunday school lesson and were in the basement changing into their choir robes. Fifteen sticks of explosives ripped through the room killing the girls, aged eleven to fourteen, and injuring twenty others as an Alabama Klan member nicknamed Dynamite Bob Chambliss watched his handiwork snuff out the young lives. The protests begun by four young students in North Carolina three years earlier had now resulted in the first child martyrs of the 1960s civil rights campaign.

While the young people who challenged the segregationist establishment generally gained at least the tacit support of many white adults, the student challenge to the university system and the American political establishment evoked much greater controversy. Almost exactly a year after the Birmingham bombing, just as the first Boomers were adapting to their freshman year in college, the academic home of the same Clark Kerr who had asserted that this college generation would be "easy" erupted in mass protest.

During the preceding few years University of California officials had allowed students to set up informational tables, solicit funds, and disseminate literature on an open lawn near Sproul Plaza on the Berkeley campus. At the start of the 1964 academic year, after remarks that the main entrance to the campus was crowded with "beatnik"-like activists, the administration revoked permission to congregate. Initial student protests turned into a "mill in," in which Manhattan College transfer and recent Mississippi civil rights activist Mario Savio and several other protesters were suspended indefinitely. On October 1 a student protest against the suspensions resulted in the arrest of former student Jack Weinberg, who was escorted to a police car that was quickly surrounded by students. During a thirty-two-hour stalemate, Savio climbed on the roof of the police car to address the crowd of protesters and emerged as the leader of a burgeoning Free Speech Movement.

President Kerr offered a series of concessions to end the stand-off temporarily, but over the next two months the concessions were revoked until Kerr announced that the administrators would press charges against Savio and seven other Free Speech Movement leaders. On December 2, 1964, a thousand students took over the Sproul Hall administration building and organized a "free university." Hours later six hundred police entered the building and conducted the

University of California student Mario Savio became the first prominent sixties student dissident when he led the Free Speech Movement at Berkeley in the fall of 1964. *(Bettmann/CORBIS)*

largest mass arrest in California history, charging eight hundred students with trespass. Many stunned faculty members declared their support for the students and for a strike they now called. On December 7 Kerr addressed a meeting of sixteen thousand faculty and students and announced a blanket clemency and liberalized policies toward student political action.

Contrary to the dreams—or nightmares—of student activists and university administrators, the Berkeley uprising remained localized in the Bay Area. Yet as the first Boomer cohort arrived at the bottom of the higher-education hierarchy in that autumn of 1964, a noticeable (if difficult to measure) enthusiasm to challenge the prescribed order of things on campus was beginning to register. One of the first tremors indicating that the times were indeed changing occurred in the music entertainment and concert scene that was an important part of college social life.

Since the emergence of Elvis Presley several years earlier, a substantial segment of the college community had found rock and roll to be less than "cool" and "cerebral," more appropriate for high schoolers and kids who did not enter higher education. The college concert and dance scene, which had been a collage of jazz, folk music, and big bands, was about to undergo a massive sea change when the first Boomers arrived.

The oldest Boomers had spent their senior year of high school entranced by the music of the Beatles and the British Invasion groups, and when they arrived in their college dorms they were little inclined to swap their music preferences for Dave Brubeck or Stan Kenton jazz. They felt quite comfortable bringing along the music of the Beatles, the Rolling Stones, or the Kinks as they reached toward young adulthood. Thus Boomer freshmen began asking for their favorite rock albums in the music section of their college bookstore, wondering why the campus radio station did not play "their" music," and clamoring for concert acts that were far less congenial to upperclassmen. No clear-cut victory would be achieved until Boomers formed the majority enrollment of each college, but it is clear that between 1964 and 1968 the college music scene was transformed from jazz to rock as a new soundtrack of the collegiate experience emerged. Along with the generational tag of the Beatles and the Rolling Stones, Bob Dylan shifted from an acoustic-guitar traditional folk singer to a more eclectic "folk rock" format, and groups such as the Byrds, the Turtles, and Sonny and Cher adapted his songs. The college Hootenanny transformed into concerts dominated by electric instruments, where audience participation songs such as "Michael, Row the Boat Ashore" became quaint artifacts of the past.

Among the skirmish points between the new students and the college administration was the continued influence of *in loco parentis* policies. American college administrators had traditionally assumed the role of surrogate parents for their late-adolescent charges as deans prescribed curfews, restrictions on mixed-gender socialization, and other policies they assumed parents would impose on children of this age at home. When the campuses were flooded with G.I. Bill recipients after World War II, college officials did their utmost to keep the twenty-something or even thirty-something veterans separated from their younger students. Now the Boomers were arriving at schools that often had stricter rules than those of their increasingly indulgent parents. By the mid-sixties, schools in urban areas with mixed student bodies of commuters and residents found that many of the "day hops" were teasing dorm residents about the school's restrictions on car ownership, nightly curfews, and enforced study halls—measures that were far stricter than their parents imposed. Some male commuters found it easier to cope with the curfew expectations of a female commuter's parents than the rigid gatekeepers positioned at the entrance to women's residence halls. The apparently arbitrary, capricious, and sometimes mean-spirited rules of *in loco parentis* in sixties colleges was a major point of contention in Boomer challenges to the academic establishment, and was often the simmering issue that ignited more broad-based confrontations and demonstrations. Students of the 1950s and early 1960s seem to have reacted to stringent university policies by surreptitiously ignoring them or accepting various sanctions as the price of doing business in the student-administration "game." Boomer students, arriving in college at a time of heightening social upheaval, found arbitrary rules simply unacceptable and were more inclined to challenge the official or system that had created them. This exasperation carried over into the sixties classroom.

Relatively fanciful books and films about the Boomer college experience in the sixties often include one or more scenes where incensed individuals or groups of students attired in "hippie-casual" clothing shout down or otherwise intimidate middle-aged professors, who are then coerced into recanting unpopular theories. This may indeed have been common in the academic chaos of Mao's Cultural Revolution in China but would have brought gasps of shock or disbelief in the classrooms of the vast majority of American colleges during this era. Contrary to some popular depictions, the vast majority of students were polite, courteous, and deferential to their professors, even in times of heightened campus activism. Still, the Boomer classroom experience provided a degree of contention that followed from the size and interpersonal nature of many classes and a grading system that was undergoing significant change.

During the fifties and early sixties most American public colleges and some private institutions had experienced a continuing expansion of faculty and student populations. Then, in 1964, the largest high school class in history graduated. Even if schools accepted the same percentage of secondary school graduates, their enrollments would increase substantially. This growth forced some schools to build more instructional facilities or stretch the school day to include early-morning and evening classes while also putting more students in each section. More and more new classroom buildings included several huge lecture halls where hundreds of students would fill multiple tiers of desks while instructors gazed upon a sea of increasingly anonymous faces.

Just as class sizes were expanding, a number of more prestigious institutions entered a form of academic arms race in which faculty now overloaded with big classes were pressed to publish books, articles, or monographs that would improve the renown of their institutions in the academic universe. While "publish or perish" was not a new term, the concept gained intensity when even mediocre institutions had visions of improving their standing. While college administrators insisted that their students would benefit from the exciting intellectual life that was part of the scholarly process, many students saw the net result as simply a difficult-to-find instructor. More college faculty members begged off from student-adviser conferences or gratefully accepted a reduced teaching load in order to concentrate on their research. Meanwhile the institution hired less-qualified graduate assistants or teaching fellows to fill the instructional gap.

This growing instructional dilemma was coupled with a sometimes erratic grading system that left many Boomers confused and angry. Recent college grading policy had revolved around the "gentleman's C," where most students would receive average grades with a few excellent marks for outstanding students and a few failures for the bottom of the class—in effect, the bell curve. But surging enrollments, governmental conscription policies, and the influx of a varied instructor corps seemed to produce more confusing rules. On the one hand, state schools that were pressured by their legislatures to expand enrollment encouraged faculty to give more failing grades, producing cumulative averages that were low enough for substantial numbers of freshmen to be dismissed from school—thus reducing the strain on the institution. On the other hand, as the war in Vietnam escalated, draft deferments were based on maintaining a 2.0 or C average. If a male student's average dropped even a fraction of a point below that level, he became eligible for military service. More than a few instructors responded to that policy, and declared their opposition to the war, by inflating grades and in some cases publicly admitting their actions. Thus the "gentleman's C" was attacked from two opposite directions. Moreover students discovered that their grades were increasingly based on impersonal machine-scored tests, with grades posted outside departmental offices by student number instead of name.

Over the long term this confluence of forces produced a gradual grade inflation at many colleges, with corresponding rises in student expectations to the point where some twenty-first-century students would view a B or B+ as a relatively average grade and sometimes insist that an A was the only reasonable reward for a course in which they had "worked very hard," regardless of test or assignment outcome. The Boomer students of the sixties would probably have eagerly accepted the grading standards applied to their children and grandchildren as they confronted an academic establishment that seemed to be encouraging a capricious grading system.

As Boomers became a majority and then a totality of undergraduate enrollment, challenging the academic establishment became linked to challenging the American government's foreign and military policies. The Vietnam War defined much of the second half of the sixties and in some way affected almost every college in the United States. Support for or opposition to the conflict varied enormously from school to school and region to region, and the Boomer student attitude was almost as varied as that of the adult population. The history of young people in the sixties might have taken very different directions if the United States had avoided massive combat in Vietnam or ended the draft before the war began. The story might have been far different again if the Boomer generation had lived through the experience of World War II America. What college students faced in the sixties was a relatively limited but media-pervasive war in which there were far more eligible males than the government needed for military service but not enough volunteers to prevent the Selective Service system from occasionally dipping into the ranks of college students.

Student reaction to the Vietnam War often ignored hard facts in favor of varying degrees of "conventional wisdom." The simple facts were that more than twenty million Boomer males turned eighteen between 1965 and 1972, and only a little more than one in ten would ever serve in Vietnam. The twelve hundred men of the Harvard class of 1968 saw only twenty-six classmates serve in Vietnam, and all returned; only two graduates of the class of 1970 reached Southeast Asia. Conscription was likely only if a student's grade fell below the magic 2.0 line or if he could not secure a graduate school, career, or medical deferment upon graduation. Yet everyone knew students who had volunteered for Vietnam or had been drafted after losing a deferment, and some of them did die in action. For much of the war, as many students faulted President Johnson for not invading North Vietnam as supported a rapid withdrawal. Other students totally supported American war policy but adamantly opposed conscription as part of that policy.

Rather than Establishment policy separating Boomers from adults, the war much more clearly divided postwar children among themselves. By 1968 many long-term friendships had foundered on the rocks of partisan politics and related attitudes toward the war. A litmus test for anything from a first date to a steady relationship was some level of harmony over attitudes on Vietnam. Sometimes collegians who agreed on their opposition to the conflict watched enmity grow as one person supported Robert Kennedy and the other Eugene McCarthy, both anti-war presidential candidates in 1968 but each seen as the "true" candidate by one faction and a fraud by their opponents.

The spring of 1968 was a season of revolt and confrontation across American campuses. Two hundred major demonstrations greeted the change of seasons, but the college that became the scene of the highest-profile media event was Columbia University in New York. The Ivy League school had one of the most politically active student bodies in the nation, as nearly five hundred of the university's three thousand undergraduates belonged to Students for a Democratic Society (SDS), a major organization of student protest. But the institution also enrolled a large number of fraternity members and was in the process of building a very good basketball team. The team's success produced an indirect spark for a campus revolution when the board of trustees voted to replace the Lions' tiny turn-of-the-century gym with a state-of-the-art arena to be constructed in university-owned Morningside Park. The park had been open for the use of the primarily minority population of adjoining Harlem neighborhoods, and SDS leaders saw a golden opportunity to forge an alliance with emerging black radical groups over the gymnasium issue.

On April 23, 1968, two hundred students occupied President Grayson Kirk's office in the Lowe Library building while militant members of the Columbia Student Afro-American

The student revolt at Columbia University in the spring of 1968 was the most prominent event in a tumultuous year of youthful challenges to the adult Establishment. Similar confrontations in France, Germany, and Mexico added an international dimension to the generation gap. *(Bettmann/CORBIS)*

Society occupied Hamilton Hall and took three white administrators hostage. In effect, two parallel occupations were under way. A large number of faculty members initially backed police attempts to enter the buildings; many of their colleagues and a substantial number of non-SDS students launched counterdemonstrations against the occupation. One of the SDS organizers, James Simon Kunen, saw the revolt as alternately serious and humorous. While admitting, "We're unhappy because of the war and because of poverty and the hopelessness of politics or because we feel lonely and alone and lost," he also took great pleasure in shaving with the president's razor and using his after-shave lotion and toothpaste, and regularly slipped out of Kirk's office to get the latest baseball scores.

The national media, however, saw little humor in a violent uprising in the wake of the assassination of Martin Luther King a few weeks earlier. *Life* magazine called it "A Great University Under Siege," observing that "Students have usurped the seat of power at Columbia University through a six-day uprising as, with the brashness of a victorious banana republic revolutionary, the mustachioed undergraduates sat in the chair of the University President and puffed on expropriated cigars. For six turbulent days the university was effectively out of business."

As supporters attempted to supply the occupiers with food and supplies, fraternity members, athletes, and others attempted to block their way. When occupation sympathizers attempted to throw food bags up toward the windows of the buildings under siege, opponents used "an improvised air defense system" of trash can lids to bring the parcels crashing to the ground. A proliferation of armbands seemed to illustrate hardening attitudes: orange among supporters, blue among opponents, green among neutral advocates of amnesty. A campus statue of Rodin's *The Thinker* soon was outfitted in all three colors as one writer suggested, "He looked as if even he was having a hard time making up his mind."

After Columbia's president sent police into the occupied buildings to clear out the students, and then dropped all charges against them, television and print media began a frenzied chronicle of student challenges to the Establishment, now increasingly labeled the "generation gap." As one writer observed, "These days the more we talk, the more we know we're a generation apart on almost everything. We're fascinated with the problem of how to get through to each other."

Although attitudes toward the Vietnam War were often based more on geographical location, family background, or academic major than on age, the "generation gap" itself was not necessarily a myth. Even students who differed violently on the war often agreed that they knew more about many issues than their frequently less-educated parents. Unlike twenty-first-century college students, who more often than not come from homes with college-educated parents, a startlingly high percentage of Boomer college students in the sixties had parents who had not even graduated from high school—a sure setting for heated dinner-table conversations. Most Boomers never occupied a campus building or were booked on police charges. Yet many of these young people looked at increasingly outdated Establishment rules and insisted that now was the time for reform. Amazingly, as Boomers pressed for change, authorities often backtracked, compromised, or waffled, setting up a future round of demands.

During the frigid, snowy winter of 1968–1969, female students in a prestigious suburban Philadelphia middle school confronted an uncomfortable reality in the sixties fashion revolution. School policy called for skirts or dresses, at a time when the mini-skirt was at the peak of popularity. As the school turned down thermostats to save energy, young women would enter the classrooms to sit on frigid plastic seats. A large number of these girls had older siblings in college, many of whom advised them to choose a day when every girl would wear pants, on the assumption that the authorities would not suspend all of them. On the appointed day, the vast majority took this advice and left their skirts at home. The principal initially balked but then conceded that, due to the cold weather, young ladies could wear pants as long as they were not jeans. For a time the victorious students happily complied. Then, several months later, a few girls wore "dressy" jeans. The remainder of the story is predictable. Challenging the Establishment in the sixties could mean anything from Jim Crow bars to a war in Southeast Asia to a seemingly capricious and outdated dress code. Yet if Boomer kids frequently argued over issues and tactics, virtually an entire generation agreed that "The Times They Are A-Changin'" was a theme song they had in common.

This questioning would produce, in the short term, an escalating level of confrontation and violence. Only a year after the "summer of love" in San Francisco extolled the virtues of peace and harmony, enraged young people and angry police officers engaged in bloody skirmishes for control of Chicago's Grant Park, which became the violent backdrop of the 1968 Democratic National Convention. As the haze of marijuana had wafted over Haight-Ashbury the summer before, the even more pungent odor of tear gas emerged as the sensory memory of Chicago. Yet if tolerance was at a premium that summer when racial and political epithets crisscrossed the bleeding nation, a new tolerance was just beginning to emerge behind the scenes. Soon white students at newly integrated Southern state universities would be lustily cheering black football and basketball players to defeat the real "adversary," their rival schools. A progression of African-American-dominated music, from soul to rap to hip-hop, would enter mainstream culture and become the music of choice for large numbers of white teens. Americans of color would move from fringe roles in television and motion pictures to a dominant presence that would rival white actors. By the early twenty-first century, star power was largely colorblind, as for most young people plot and action trumped the racial or ethnic backgrounds of the stars.

The challenge to the Establishment that reached a crescendo of violence in Grant Park in the summer of 1968 would reach a far more peaceful and momentous climax four decades later in exactly the same location. On an unseasonably warm night in November 2008, an enormous crowd occupied Grant Park. Yet this time police officers merely acknowledged the people with smiles and waves. Unlike in 1968, the participants represented a wide range of Americans, from tiny infants to citizens who had already been middle-aged forty years earlier. African Americans, Latinos, Asian Americans, and whites mixed easily, their most visible commonality being campaign buttons supporting a candidate for the American presidency. Then, after a momentary hush at 10 P.M. Central Time, a twenty-four-hour television satellite news channel (a media venue that would have been almost unthinkable forty years earlier) projected that the candidate favored by these onlookers had effectively won the presidency. The rock throwing and clubbing of 1968 were replaced by warm embraces, which included many of the men and women in blue. Finally, in the last hours of that momentous November 4, a rather young man who had known the sixties only as a child harkened back to the positive accomplishments of that tumultuous decade as he made his first speech as the newly elected president of a nation that had begun to grow more tolerant and accepting in the Boomer era.

\\\|//
10

THE SUMMER OF '69
AND BEYOND

THE SUMMER OF 1939 was probably the most pleasant in-
terlude in the often grim decade of the thirties, and the upbeat mood included the nation's children and adolescents.
Parents and children lined up to see *The Wizard of Oz*, and
more than a few viewers sat mesmerized as the rather bleak
black-and-white landscape of Dorothy's Kansas was transformed into the stunning color of the Emerald City. Children at municipal pools and local swimming holes congre-
gated to listen to Little Orphan Annie on the radio and saw
the latest installments of the Andy Hardy and Nancy Drew
movies in theaters that promised an air-conditioned escape
from the heat.

The single largest concentration of young people on
any given day that summer was in Flushing Meadows, New
York, where the most spectacular World's Fair in history had
grabbed the nation's attention. The theme of the exposition
was "The World of Tomorrow," which explored visions of
American life in the distant 1960s. To reach the fair, parents,

teenagers, and children boarded special runs of the Broadway Limited or Southern Crescent trains, climbed into nar-
row berths, or fidgeted in day coaches as the world of the
late 1930s sped by. Then, almost like Dorothy's entry to Oz,
the pavilions of the World's Fair loomed on the skyline. Boys
in shirts and ties with slicked-back hair and girls with styl-
ish hats, gloves, and Mary Jane shoes gasped in excitement
as they were offered a taste of a 1960s world of television,
superhighways, and monorails. Then this brief escape from
the still-grinding economic downturn ended as summer gave
way to a sober autumn in which Europe plunged into war.
As Hitler's legions swept across the Continent, one by one
the lights of foreign pavilions darkened forever, and Americans prepared for the grim possibility of war.

Three decades later the children of those excited young
people who sampled the 1960s at Flushing Meadows would
celebrate the last summer of the sixties in very different
ways. Transistor radios and car speakers blasted out songs
that would have shocked the kids of 1939. Two of the most
frequently played songs, "Hair" and "Aquarius/Let the Sunshine In," were taken from the smash Broadway musical
Hair, whose suggestive language and nudity would have
landed the producers and actors in jail thirty years earlier.

The children of 1969 had access to the video entertainment world promised at Flushing Meadows, but on a much
grander scale than those World's Fair visitors could ever
have imagined. Most children now had access to televisions
double or triple the screen size imagined in 1939, with color
sets largely replacing black-and-white, and new enterprises
such as cable networks and the Public Broadcasting System
offering a growing variety of attractions designed specifically
for children.

The sleek superhighways envisioned in 1939 were now a reality, easing travel and vacations for Boomer children and their parents. The train experience was now largely the automobile experience as the rear seat of a car replaced the day coach as a child's vantage point for viewing the American landscape.

If Flushing Meadows was the epicenter of a young person's imagination in the summer of 1939, two locations transfixed attention three decades later. The first event, which began on Cape Kennedy, Florida, in a large sense fulfilled the promise of the World of Tomorrow. On July 20, 1969, the U.S. spacecraft Apollo XI landed on the moon, and Neil Armstrong turned the fantasy world of Buck Rogers into a reality when he became the first human to step onto an extraterrestrial world. John F. Kennedy had begun the sixties with a call for space travel; Neil Armstrong had ended the decade with the validation of that dream. For a moment, on that sultry summer evening, the generation gap briefly ended as small children, teenagers, college students, parents, and senior citizens huddled around flickering television sets sharing feelings of trepidation, relief, joy, and excitement for the long-awaited event.

Virtually everyone in America could understand and appreciate the accomplishments of the intrepid Apollo XI crew when Armstrong, followed by Buzz Aldrin, stepped down the ladder to the moon's chalky surface in what he called "one small step for a man, one giant leap for mankind." If members of the Greatest Generation equated the event with the 1930s adventures of Flash Gordon, Boomers sensed it was almost like a moment from *Star Trek*. Both age groups could agree that this was a moment in their lives to be remembered long after the Apollo program had ended.

The location of the other defining, if more controversial, event of the summer of 1969 was a muddy farm owned by Max Yasgur near the little town of Bethel, New York. There a group of promoters planned an event that, on the surface, sounded like a miniature version of the Flushing Meadows event of three decades earlier. They advertised the Woodstock Music and Art Fair: An Aquarian Exposition, a festival that at first glance might attract visitors from a variety of age groups. Instead of offering stately pavilions for well-dressed visitors, however, the promoters hoped to attract fifty thousand young people at eighteen dollars per person to hear Janis Joplin; Jimi Hendrix; Joan Baez; The Who; The Grateful Dead; Crosby, Stills, Nash and Young; and numerous other groups that defined Boomer popular music at the end of the sixties.

A turnout of fifty thousand for a concert on a rural thousand-acre farm would have been an impressive social event with substantial profits. As it turned out, the organizers received both more and less than they expected. Even before Jimi Hendrix played his spectacularly edgy version of "The Star-Spangled Banner," a youth pilgrimage was under way. As roads clogged in the most massive traffic jam in the Empire State's history, the first wave of arrivals was surging onto the grounds, knocking down fences and generally avoiding paying any admission charge. Three days of sultry heat punctuated by seemingly endless thunderstorms turned the venue into a sea of mud where a crowd nearly ten times the expected attendance banged on tambourines, sang, played songs, and shared food, drinks, and more than a few varieties of drugs.

Thirty years earlier Flushing Meadows had been filled with rather formally dressed young people sharing a vision

The "Aquarian Exposition" staged at Max Yasgur's dairy farm attracted more than ten times as many participants as expected. In some respects Woodstock was a final celebration of sixties youth culture as the realities of career choices, parental responsibilities, and the economic downturn of the seventies emerged. *(Henry Diltz/CORBIS)*

of the future with their parents and grandparents. Now, in 1969, young people had created the third-largest city in New York virtually overnight, and, sometimes without any clothes at all, they were sharing a very different vision with one another in a community almost devoid of adults.

Woodstock became the largest single gathering of Boomers that generation would ever experience, and there is little doubt that the postwar babies dominated the event. The oldest Boomers were now twenty-three and entering a transition between childhood and adulthood that was held in suspended animation for three days. The most visible contingent of pre-Boomer-era participants was made up of the members of the performing bands who had largely become the muses of the new generation. The performers, more than a few of whom would be dead before thirty, and their

Boomer audience shared a vision of a future in which technological advances seemed relatively unimportant. As singer Joni Mitchell preached, "We are stardust, we are golden, and we've got to get ourselves back to the garden." Many of those soggy pilgrims sensed that at least for a brief period they were living in a world outside adult jurisdiction and rules, where sharing a sleeping bag could also mean sharing sexual partners, and the smoky haze drifting upward would not provoke adult sanctions. Even if most Boomers could not be physically present at Woodstock Nation, the turnout was so huge it seemed that "everyone" was there, especially to adults who tried to understand such a spontaneous event.

Beyond the mystique of Woodstock, the summer of 1969 represents a seminal moment in the Boomer childhood experience. At this point the largest percentage of the generation was composed of fully aware individuals who still occupied some form of dependent state required in any definition of childhood. The largest number of Boomers that would ever be enrolled in school was now getting ready to return to classrooms ranging from kindergarten to graduate school. Soon older Boomers would be leaving school faster than the youngest Boomers would replace them, and the 1970s would become an era of laid-off teachers, closed schools, and shrinking class size. In 1969 the large families of the Boomer era were still represented in the blended six-child family of *The Brady Bunch*, an enormously popular representation of the entire generation. If Woodstock was an iconic moment for Boomers who were about to become adults, the adventures of Greg and Marsha and their siblings showed a continuity of the childhood and family experience that dated to *The Donna Reed Show* and *Leave It to Beaver*, with the added attraction of six kids rather than two.

The autumn of 1969 also featured a series of domestic and foreign policy initiatives that, after a final flare-up of youth demonstrations, would gradually weaken the cultural and generational divide over the Vietnam War. Richard Nixon had run his successful 1968 presidential campaign on a promise of "peace with honor," implying that the Vietnam conflict could be ended without American defeat. In the short term, the realization that the United States would not withdraw from Vietnam in the near future mobilized the most extensive and at times most violent youth opposition to the conflict. In the summer of 1969 the national convention of Students for a Democratic Society turned into a near brawl as the organization splintered into rival factions, each proclaiming itself the true believers of a national revolution. The most radical faction emerged as the Weathermen, who took their name from the lines of a Bob Dylan song, "You don't need a weatherman to know which way the wind blows." By October the Weathermen had assembled several hundred members in Chicago with the promise to "bring the war home" through vandalism, running battles with police, and domestic terrorism centered on a bombing campaign of schools and agencies that were accused of supporting the war. Weathermen leaders, such as Bernardine Dohrn and Mark Rudd, went underground as SDS itself devolved into ever smaller factions.

As SDS imploded, a new anti-war coalition, the Vietnam Moratorium Committee, formed around student government leaders, clergy, and Vietnam veterans who opposed the war. On October 15, 1969, the Committee sponsored a day of protests including demonstrations, vigils, and teach-ins in a great many communities, which included the participation of a number of children of senior Nixon administration officials. Four weeks later nearly a half-million demonstrators descended on Washington in the largest protest of the war. Yet just as this anti-war movement reached its greatest breadth of support and legitimacy, a series of administration initiatives and legislative priorities began to dampen the mood of protest. First, Nixon announced a plan of "Vietnamization," in which South Vietnam troops would progressively replace American forces in combat. This allowed a series of ever larger troop withdrawals along with reduced American casualties. Second, the president and Congress largely agreed to replace conscription with volunteer armed forces and to reduce the voting age from twenty-one to eighteen. Finally, until the draft was fully ended a lottery system would be initiated in which young men would be subject to call for only a single year and virtually assured of exemption if their lottery number was higher than Selective Service estimates for the coming year.

On a cold, early-December night in 1969, millions of male Boomers gathered around transistor radios or watched television to learn the matchup of birthdates and lottery numbers. For perhaps a third of these young men, their low numbers were a signal to prepare for conscription, enter the National Guard, or find a career that provided exemption from the draft. The remaining two-thirds were essentially given permission to go on with their lives in a society where Vietnam was gradually receding as a focal point of the Boomer experience. These older Boomers now joined their younger counterparts in an environment in which the Vietnam War was primarily a television image rather than a personal reality.

The draft lottery represented one of the two last communal Boomer experiences of the sixties, and, as with many

In the wake of disorders at the 1968 Democratic Convention, the trial of the Chicago 7 and the continuation of the Vietnam War into 1969 provided the catalyst for massive student protests, like the Weathermen's "Days of Rage" in Chicago. *(Getty Images)*

events of the decade, evoked varied emotions, depending upon whether an individual "won" or "lost." A similar mix of emotions emerged at about the same time when a group of California promoters tried to stage a West Coast version of Woodstock. In an attempt to counter charges they had surrendered to commercialism, the Rolling Stones offered to give a free concert at Altamont Speedway. When top-tier groups such as the Grateful Dead, Santana, and Jefferson Airplane signed on for the show, nearly 300,000 fans descended on the Speedway, a site only one-sixth as large as Max Yasgur's farm. As huge numbers of fans ringed the hillside above the stage and attempted to listen to the bands, the throng nearest the stage pushed and shoved against a security screen dominated by the dubious law enforcement of a phalanx of Hell's Angels motorcyclists. When Mick Jagger began the first part of the controversial song "Sympathy for the Devil," a small-time hoodlum pulled a gun and was immediately surrounded by Angels, one of whom stabbed him to death. Fans at a distance remembered Altamont primarily for the music while stage-side participants left with images of mayhem.

As the lottery and Altamont put a period to a raucous decade, Boomers and their seniors wondered how the new decade might resemble the recent past. One national magazine suggested, "There is no spelled-out forecast for the new decade because the unpredictable 1960s cracked the crystal ball too badly and proved that all we can prophesy with certainty is change. The 1960s shook us all so deeply that few easy assumptions can still be made about our basic beliefs, about our opinions of ourselves, about our social divisions, fears or hopes." No one could predict how many Boomers would keep the fifties and sixties of their childhood in their memories, if not on their calendars.

In the summer of 1973, as the Vietnam experience faded and the turmoil of Watergate appeared, a young producer named George Lucas released a film that chronicled the experiences of a small group of teenagers on one night in the Kennedy era. As posters filled movie theaters with the tantalizing question, "Where were you in '62?" huge audiences followed largely unknown actors—Ron Howard, Cindy Williams, McKenzie Phillips, Harrison Ford, and Richard Dreyfus—as they negotiated the teen experience in small-town California. Lucas used most of his budget for the nonstop soundtrack that opens with a booming rendition of "Rock Around the Clock" outside a classic drive-in restaurant and closes with the Beach Boys' "All Summer Long" as Dreyfus boards a plane to leave his family and friends behind on his way to an Eastern college. As the 1973 audience remarked to one another on the short hair of the boys and the conservative dresses worn by the girls in 1962, more than a few viewers sensed the nostalgia of the passing of an era. Soon the success of *American Graffiti* spawned the television hits *Happy Days* and *Laverne and Shirley* and the musical nostalgia of Billy Joel and other singers. "Fifties" and "sixties" theme parties and dances drew large crowds of high school and college students, now increasingly made up of younger Boomers anxious to feel vicariously the excitement of their older siblings at a time when young people seemed on their way to dominating American culture. These younger Boomers would have their own dreams and their own memories, and as the millennium approached, retro "disco" and "seventies" events would evoke the same laughter and nostalgia in this younger cohort who had never experienced *Howdy Doody* or the original Mousketeers but could name every character on *The Brady Bunch*. The generation of children who had known Sputnik, Camelot, and the Beatles were now becoming parents of their own children. Younger Boomers were about to make the dawning seventies their own time.

11

A GOOD TIME TO GROW UP

THE END of the 1960s marked the climax of a fascinating and influential era in the history of American childhood and youth culture. Many of the older Boomers were making the transition from student to worker and parent, perhaps wondering whether their generational warning to "not trust anyone over thirty" would apply to themselves, for that milestone loomed just over half a decade away. Meanwhile, behind the older Boomers were tens of millions of younger postwar children who would enter the seventies as preschoolers. They were *Brady Bunch* children, not members of Howdy Doody's Peanut Gallery, and their childhood and adolescence would be influenced by disco, *Star Wars*, Atari games, and MTV. If the older Boomers' classes were interrupted by news of John Kennedy's assassination, the younger Boomers' classroom television sets would be tuned to the Watergate hearings.

Postwar children who were old enough to experience a substantial portion of the fifties and sixties would spend much of the next few decades trying to understand their experience and how it jibed with broader depictions of the era. Much of my purpose in this book has been to frame the period in terms of its particular perspectives. When the template is configured to include the experiences of typical, average participants in the fifties and sixties, a number of realities may be seen.

First, the Boomer generation grew up at a time when adult society was more interested in the activities of the nation's young people than in most other eras. From Benjamin Spock's best-selling book on babies to late-sixties adults adopting many of the fashions and hairstyles of their children, kid-watching became a national pastime. Just as seventeenth-century Puritan family portraits depict children as miniature adults, with scaled-down adult clothing and facial expressions, 1960s snapshots of teenage daughters *and* their mothers attired in blue jeans, and middle-aged fathers displaying the same long sideburns and wide belts as their sons, provide a visual clue that many adults closely watched the cultural activities of their children, and sometimes not so secretly envied them.

Second, it seems probable that most postwar children recognized their status as members of a huge numerical cohort relatively early in their childhood, and that more often than not they viewed this phenomenon as a blessing rather than a curse. Contemporary articles and my own interviews suggest that Boomers viewed their situation with anything from bemused acceptance to outright delight. Sharing bunk beds, cramped bedrooms, and playthings often became a virtual badge of honor, not unlike the "we can take it" pride of Londoners who endured the German Blitz. If the Boomer experience often meant that cakes and pizzas had to be sliced into smaller portions, it also provided a much greater assortment of potential playmates and friends in the neighborhood. A child seeking a "best friend" with compatible attributes did not have to venture far to locate a likely candidate. The pool was often so large that a child could locate multiple "best friends," which conveniently offered spare candidates in case of periodic disruptions.

Third, the emergence of the first young "television generation" proved to be quite different from what pessimistic critics or euphoric supporters of TV imagined. Boomers were the first generation of children exposed to the influence of television, and there is little doubt that many children did their homework on the living-room floor in front of a television, were sometimes more likely to watch a flickering video screen than read a good book, and spent more time memorizing the characters of TV Westerns than the multiplication tables. On the other hand, as late as the end of the sixties the average child had access to a television that carried only three or four channels, only a tiny fraction of twenty-first-century counterparts. Most contemporary accounts and interviews with Boomers indicate that they loved television, had numerous favorite programs, and watched far more late-night, adult-oriented shows than their parents either knew about or admitted. But in summer, on weekends, and in late afternoons many children preferred outdoor play to television viewing, and even at night the television provided mainly background noise as friends or family played Scrabble, Monopoly, or Game of Life, or enjoyed their toys. In fact, television often encouraged children to read more about the topic of a program. If TV was often distracting, it also could expand children's horizons in ways undreamed of even a generation earlier, and as the sixties ended it was clear that television was not about to recede as a major factor in the childhood experience.

Fourth, as the title of this book indicates, the children of this era are clearly the definitive "cold-war generation." The all-encompassing reality of growing up in the quarter-century after World War II was the apparently permanent state of hostility and confrontation between the United States and the Communist bloc, led by the Soviet Union and supported by the People's Republic of China. Historians dealing with this period may argue over who initiated the cold war, how close civilization came to a nuclear Armageddon, and whether the confrontation was avoidable, but there is little argument that the cold war permeated American life.

Children of this era grew acclimated to the rhythms of the confrontation through numerous civil defense films, the "duck and cover" activities of the animated Bert the Turtle, and weekly air raid drills. Boomers wondered what would happen if a nuclear attack found them at school and separated from their parents, or on a bike ride home. Terms such as "fallout" and "radiation" were as familiar as "hopscotch" and "Wiffle ball." Illustrated magazines on the living room coffee table provided photo essays on how to build a backyard fallout shelter and showed children playing board games in a basement crammed with survival gear.

On television the cold war sometimes offered more real-life drama than Westerns or action shows. The kindly, grandfatherly demeanor of Dwight Eisenhower and the youth, vigor, and determination of John Kennedy contrasted with the shoe-pounding threats of "We will bury you" from the menacing Nikita Khrushchev. If all the Boomers did not experience a Pearl Harbor or a 9/11, they endured a much longer period of vague threat punctuated by the major crises of Sputnik and the Cuban Missile Crisis.

Yet just as Pearl Harbor and the World Trade Center produced positive emotions of solidarity, generosity, and personal sacrifice, the Boomer experience with the cold war was not uniformly negative. The initial shock of Sputnik gave way to more positive emotions in the building of model kits of the orbiting craft, construction of cardboard rockets in school classrooms, and the heightened availability of space helmets and futuristic play clothes in stores. If *Twilight Zone* episodes dealing with nuclear war were sobering, the activities of the Mercury, Gemini, and Apollo astronauts were breathtaking. This book ends just after the triumphant landing of Apollo XI effectively "won" the space-race component of the cold war.

These four provable realities of the Boomer childhood experience between 1946 and 1969 make it one of the best eras for growing up in America. Taking into account the implications of ongoing (if gradually diminishing) racial discrimination, gender bias, religious tensions, and ethnic exclusion, the period nonetheless was a genuinely positive time for most Boomers.

The children of the postwar era grew up in a period when the economic distress, dislocation, hardship, and lack of parental supervision of the depression and World War II had largely ended. Prosperity was sufficiently widespread that a reasonably comfortable lifestyle could be had with the earnings of one parent if the other chose to stay home. While some women did grow bored and unfulfilled in their roles as full-time housewives and mothers, the culture of the time certainly reinforced the vital importance of their contributions, and there is every suspicion that most children who lived in a home with a mother as homemaker had no desire to trade places with their friends who had two working parents. Many homemaker mothers were involved with much more than shopping lists and meal preparations. They joined PTAs, served as den mothers or Girl Scout advisers, and volunteered for charity drives, all of which directly or indirectly had a positive effect on their children. On the other hand, if Boomer children were generally insulated from the dislocation and economic distress of the 1930s and early 1940s, they often grew up before the soaring divorce rate, the rise in out-of-wedlock births, and the economic necessity of two working parents turned the late twentieth and early twenty-first centuries into a sometimes lonely and confusing experience. The children of this more contemporary era have sometimes been defined as "a tribe apart" as they confront blended families, parents working extended hours, and a world in which iPods, text messaging, and the internet often replace personal contact.

There is no "best" or "worst" time to be a child. The spectrum of childhood experience in any era exhibits a sometimes horrifying range between happiness and terror. Many Boomers who were old enough to experience the fifties and sixties in some form quickly adopted a special feeling about the fashion, the films, the music, and the attitudes of the these decades almost as soon as they ended. Boomers who were barely adults themselves looked sourly at disco, seventies television, and new fashions, and searched for the "good old days" in Oldies radio stations, *Happy Days* on television, and *Grease* on stage and screen. Yet as nostalgia swept through one part of the Boomer generation during the seventies, millions of their younger siblings and neighbors saw only magic in the newly dawning era. But that experience is another story.

A NOTE ON SOURCES

THE PERIOD from 1946 to 1969 quite probably witnessed the peak influence of mass-circulation magazines and journals in the United States, and many families were affluent enough to subscribe to a broad range of them. The media domination of cable television and the internet was still to come. Substantial elements of this book were gleaned from hundreds of period journals. An almost mandatory activity in a project of this nature is the investigation of *Life* and *Look*, the two major mass-circulation magazines of the era. While both of these periodicals contain the celebrity orientation of modern journals such as *People* and *Us*, they also presented serious discussions of the national and international scene and focused heavily on contemporary family life, parenthood, and childhood experiences. Coupled with their extensive, largely full-color advertisements, these two periodicals provide priceless glimpses into the daily world of the Boomers and their families.

The major news weeklies of the era are invaluable for their chronicles of important events of the period. *Time* and *Newsweek* provide an excellent narrative of primary news events while *U.S. News* offers substantially more material on school issues, parenting concerns, the economic and social impact of the Baby Boom, and projections of future trends in society. Several other general-audience periodicals proved surprisingly valuable. *Fortune* magazine featured highly readable assessments of the economic and marketing aspects of the ongoing population explosion and included several multi-issue predictions about life in America in both the 1980s and the early twenty-first century. *Sports Illustrated* varied its nuts-and-bolts reports on sporting events with articles on the role of sports in all levels of education and the impact of race and gender changes in sports on the broader society. *T.V. Guide* offered far more than grids that highlighted television programming for a particular week in a particular year. It also featured extensive articles on the impact of television violence on young children, the possible effect of global television on education, and the future role of adult Boomers when they became the gatekeepers for their children's viewing experiences.

The role of children in families and the broader adult society seemed to be a perennial theme in mass-market women's magazines such as *Redbook, Ladies' Home Journal,* and *Good Housekeeping.* "Back to School" child fashion layouts were interspersed with features on discipline, social and school success, and the shared responsibilities of mothers and fathers. Even *Better Homes and Gardens* offered features on coping with overcrowding in new suburban houses and hints on managing the issues of shared bedrooms and study spaces. *Parents* magazine at times seemed almost, but not quite, a women's journal, as it conceded that mothers spent far more time with their children than fathers. But it carried just enough features on joint parents' concerns and the special roles of the male parent to provide a slightly different perspective than more general periodicals.

Two valuable references aimed at child readers were *Jack and Jill* and the *Mickey Mouse Club Magazine.* The former magazine offers excellent insights into the stories, games, and activities that were approved by parents of the time. Disney's offering features fascinating features on the relationship of 1950s children to young people of yesterday and tomorrow. In fact the initial article in the first issue in 1956 featured two children and their parents preparing to celebrate New Year 2000, and comparing their lifestyles to those of their counterparts nearly five decades earlier. While the feature provided only mixed results in the accuracy of its predictions, it offered an excellent perspective on how child Boomers may have perceived their adult future.

The world of preteen and teenage girls of the era received massive coverage in *Seventeen* and *Glamour*, both of which explored attitudes about relationships, popularity, school issues, and career prospects. Equivalent sources for a male Boomer perspective are more difficult to find. Boys' attitudes about adolescence must often be filtered through indirect sources, such as the enormously popular DC and Marvel comic books and satire magazines such as *Mad* and *Cracked*, with proper allowance for the nature of these publications.

While contemporary periodicals proved invaluable to the research for this book, some fifty contemporary and later books added greater perspective. A number of excellent general histories of the fifties and sixties were written between the early 1970s and the early 1990s. Works on the earlier decade include Douglas Miller and Marion Novak, *The Fifties the Way They Really Were* (New York, 1977); J. Ronald Oakley, *God's Country: America in the Fifties* (New York, 1986); William L. O'Neill, *American High: The Years of Confidence* (New York, 1986); and the magisterial David Halberstam work, *The Fifties* (New York, 1993), which is a necessity for gaining a full appreciation of the decade. Works on the 1960s include William L. O'Neill, *Coming Apart: An Informal History of America in the 1960's* (Chicago, 1971); David Faber, *The Age of Great Dreams: America in the 1960s* (New York, 1974); and Joseph Peter, *An Oral History of the 1960s* (New York, 1974).

These works offer some contrasts with the longer-term perspective from the twenty-first century, including Stuart Kallen, *The 1950s* (San Diego, 2000); Mark Lytle, *America's Uncivil Wars: The Sixties Era from Elvis to the Fall of Richard Nixon* (New York, 2006); Karen Mannus Smith and Tim Koster, *The Time It Was* (Saddle River, N.J., 2008); and Michael Kazin, *America Divided* (New York, 2008). These authors generally view the 1950s as less conservative and the 1960s as less radical than their earlier predecessors.

Chapters on the emergence of Boomer families and 1950s home life begin with reference to Dr. Benjamin Spock, *The Common Sense Book of Baby and Child Care* (New York, 1946). I believe it is difficult to overestimate Spock's influence on early postwar child-rearing. Lynn White, *Educating Our Daughters* (New York,

1950) provides another valuable contemporary insight into the experience of parenthood while Thomas Hine, *Populuxe: The Life and Look of America in the 1950s and 1960s* (New York, 1986) is a lavishly illustrated view of home life in the era. More recent works on this topic include Stephanie Coontz, *Marriage: A History* (New York, 2005) and Peter Stearns, *Anxious Parents: A History of Modern Childrearing in America* (New York, 2003). Steve Gillon, *Boomer Nation* (New York, 2004) provides interesting demographic aspects in a work that concentrates on the emergence of the Boomer generation as adults.

Chronicles of the teenage experiences of Boomers and their older siblings cover a wide spectrum of publication dates. Contemporary accounts include James Herlihy, *Blue Denim* (New York, 1959) and Enid Haupt, *The Seventeen Book of Young Living* (New York, 1957); more recent treatments include Thomas Hine, *The Rise and Fall of the American Teenager* (New York, 1999) and Kate Burns, *The American Teenager* (Farmington, Mich., 2003).

The impact of school overcrowding, the cold war, and Sputnik on American schools and children was a major feature of contemporary books. These include Albert Lynd, *Quackery in the Public Schools* (Boston, 1953); Rudolf Flesch, *Why Johnny Can't Read* (New York, 1955); and the less shrill and more prescriptive James Conant, *The American High School Today* (New York, 1959). Two excellent perspectives on the impact of Sputnik on the Boomer experiences are Paul Dickson, *Sputnik: Shock of the Century* (New York, 2000) and Homer Hickam, Jr., *The Rocket Boys* (New York, 1999). Joel Spring, *The Sorting Machine* (New York, 1976) chronicles the broader topic of utilizing Boomer children as an asset in cold-war policymaking.

The popular culture of the Boomers is a well-chronicled element of the postwar narrative. Joel Whitburn, *The Top Ten Single Charts of Billboard Magazine: 1955–2000* (Menominee, Wisc., 2001) is an invaluable guide to the type of music that Boomers and their older siblings found exciting during the period. Glenn Altschuler, *All Shook Up: How Rock and Roll Changed America* (New York, 2003) and Ed Ward, Geoffrey Stokes and Ken Tucker, *Rock of Ages: The Rolling Stone History of Rock and Roll* (New York, 1986) explain the cultural impact of the new music on teenagers. Thomas Doherty, *Teenagers and Teenpics* (Boston, 1986) and Karal Ann Martling, *As Seen on T.V.: The Visual Culture of Everyday Life in the 1950s* (Cambridge, Mass., 1994) evaluates the impact of film and television on Boomers from the perspective of a later time while Robert Shayon, *Television and Our Children* (New York, 1951) views the topic from the early days of the postwar culture.

The drama of challenging the Establishment in the civil rights and student activism movements has received substantial coverage. The emotionally wrenching saga of the integration of Little Rock Central High School is chronicled in Melba Banks, *Warriors Don't Cry* (New York, 1984). Henry Hampton and Steve Fayer offer a wider lens on the movement in *Voices of Freedom: An Oral History of the Civil Rights Movement* (New York, 1991), which in turn complements Robert Weisbrot's *Freedom Bound* (New York, 1990).

The New Left on the college campus receives extensive treatment in James Simon Kunen, *The Strawberry Statement: Notes of a College Revolutionary* (New York, 1968) and Todd Gitlin, *The Sixties: Years of Hope, Days of Rage* (New York, 1987). Conservative culture in confrontation is a major element of John Andrew, *The Other Side of the Sixties* (New York, 1997) and Mary Brennan, *Turning Right in the Sixties* (New York, 1995). An excellent, balanced narrative of student activism is Kenneth Heineman, *Put Your Bodies Upon the Wheels* (Chicago, 2001).

Narratives of the Boomer experience in the crucial year of 1968 include Jules Witcover, *The Year the Dream Died: Revisiting America in 1968* (New York, 1998) and Mark Kurlansky, *1968—The Year That Rocked the World* (New York, 2004). The cultural transition from the end of the sixties to the dawn of a new decade is a major topic of Theodore Roszak, *The Making of a Counter Culture* (New York, 1969) and Michael Doyle, *Imagine Nation: The American Counterculture of the 1960s and 1970s* (New York, 2002).

INDEX

McCarthy, Eugene, 159
McCartney, Paul, 106, 132
Mickey Mouse Club, 63, 80, 82, 184
Motion pictures, 13, 66, 80, 96, 105, 163
Movies, 13–15, 40, 67, 70–71, 86, 111, 133, 165; comedy, 68, 91; horror, 105, science fiction, 87

NBC, 62, 140, 143
Nelson, Ricky, 83, 90
New Frontier, 97, 119, 133
Nixon, Richard, 171, 185
Normandy invasion, 43
North Carolina A&T College, 145–147

Pacific War, 102
Pearl Harbor, 3, 5, 10, 16, 19, 52, 179–180
Plastic, 69, 71, 103, 162; "age of," 40
Presley, Elvis, 78–79, 81, 88–89, 153

Radio, 4–5, 13–15, 39–40, 54, 59–60, 68, 80, 87, 89, 109, 153; programs, 70, 84, 165, 181
Rock-and-roll, 105–107; music, 80–81, 84, 87–89
Rolling Stones, 140, 153, 173
Roosevelt, Franklin, 5

Salk, Jonas, 38
Savio, Mario, 120, 151–152
Schools: American, 54, 99, 186
Serviceman's Readjustment Act, 19–20, 27
Seventeen magazine, 79
Sit-ins, 146–148
Sixteenth Street Baptist Church, 149–150
Soviet Union, 51–54, 100, 138, 142, 179
Spock, Benjamin, 19, 22–24, 38, 43, 144, 177, 185; "Spock babies," 96, 120
Sputnik, 71, 98, 116, 135, 175, 179–180, 186; launch, ix, 54–56
Star Trek, 143, 167
Suburban, 46, 110, 184; community, 24, 35, 48, 111; development, 26, 28, 30; living, 31, 33, 67, 140; models, x, 30–32
Sullivan, Ed, 81, 132

Technology, ix, 41, 48–49, 55, 87
Teenagers, 86, 88–92, 99, 102–103, 111, 115–116, 166–167, 174; preteen, 40, 78, 86, 88–91, 103, 106, 110–112, 185
Television stations, 14, 66
Thirties, 15, 59, 66, 69, 74–75, 165
Tobacco, 11–12